THE COMPLETE GUIDE TO

RESIDENTIAL DECK CONSTRUCTION

THE COMPLETE GUIDE TO

RESIDENTIAL DECK CONSTRUCTION

From the Simplest to the Most Sophisticated

GREG ROY

BETTERWAY PUBLICATIONS, INC.
WHITE HALL, VIRGINIA

Published by Betterway Publications, Inc.
P.O. Box 219
Crozet, VA 22932
(804) 823-5661

Cover and text photos courtesy of Archadeck
Typography by Park Lane Associates

Library of Congress Cataloging-in-Publication Data

Roy, Greg
The complete guide to residential deck construction : from the simplest to the most sophisticated / Greg Roy.
p. cm.
Includes index.
ISBN 1-55870-231-8
1. Decks (Architecture, Domestic)--Design and construction--amateurs' manuals. I. Title.
TH4970.R64 1992
690'.89--dc20 91-43108
CIP

Printed in the United States of America
0 9 8 7 6 5 4 3 2 1

To my best friend and the sweetest person in the world,
Carol Roy.

Acknowledgments

I am fortunate to have dear friends and colleagues who offered much support and encouragement to me as I created this book; without them, this book would not exist.

A special thanks goes to R. Dodge Woodson, who introduced me to the field of writing and also to the publisher of this book. He has been a personal walking encyclopedia to me.

Gary Roy, my brother and business partner, deserves much credit for carrying an additional workload to allow me the hours needed to write this book. Thanks, Gary.

Pastor Darrel Taylor—I admire his integrity and dedication to truth—has been a genuine friend and has provided more encouragement than I can express.

There are many others who contributed in some way to this book. In alphabetical order, some of them are the Audette family; my sister, Linda Black; Richard Caron; the Leo family; the Ludington family; my parents; and the remainder of the Taylor family, including Mrs. Pastor, Jesse, and Aaron. Thank you to all of you.

Contents

1
Evaluating Your Deck Needs

Whether you're cooking a Friday evening barbecue, reading the newspaper outside on a sunny Saturday morning, or relaxing in the cool afternoon shade, your deck is—or should be—one of your yard's major attractions. With careful planning and forethought, your deck will become the centerpiece of your home's outdoor activities.

As you begin the planning process, you must look at your deck project from many different angles. This will help you clearly understand all the various factors that make the difference between a great deck and a white elephant. Just as the three most important factors in real estate are location, location, and location, the three most important factors affecting your deck are planning, planning, and planning.

WHY DO YOU WANT A DECK?

The first question to be answered as you start to formulate ideas is why do you want to have a deck? What activities will it accommodate? This is the very basic starting point in planning and designing a deck perfectly suited to your lifestyle. All these questions are recorded in checklist form, in the Appendix. You will benefit by copying those pages and answering in detail the questions they contain. The checklists will become a reference you will use over and over as you make your way through the maze of the planning process.

Among the activities to consider are eating and cooking. Will you be using your deck for family cookouts? If so, will you be doing the cooking on the deck or in another location? Your eating location should be sheltered from the smoke of the barbecue. Will these cookouts be primarily for your own family, or do you regularly have friends or relatives join you for a meal? If much of the time others will be invited over, then you will want to provide enough space on your deck to accommodate comfortably your family as well as guests.

Will your cooking be done on a portable gas or charcoal grill, or would you like a brick or stone barbecue pit built into your deck? If a permanent barbecue pit is more than your budget will allow, would you like to design a special place for your portable grill? Planning a location for it will make cooking out that much easier and more enjoyable. You will not have to go to your garage, basement, or storage area and carry the grill to the deck—it will already be there. You may even decide that you want a weathertight storage area for barbecue accessories. Think of the convenience of having charcoal, utensils, paper plates, and other items right next to your grill. If you like this idea, plan it into your design.

You must also consider seating in your planning process. You may decide to purchase patio furniture as an alternative to one of the many bench designs illustrated in Chapter 9. After the checklist on planning is completed, it should be clear which alternative will be best for you—built-in, purchased, or a combination of the two.

Besides cooking and eating, what other activities do you want your deck to accommodate? Do you have young children? Do they often play outside? Would you like a fence-type railing surrounding the perimeter of your deck? This could form an enclosed play area that is safe for youngsters. Do you want a built-in sandbox for your child? These questions and others are included on the checklist. They will help you determine the components necessary to include in your deck to make it meet your special needs.

WHERE TO LOCATE YOUR DECK

Once your checklists are completed, consider where to locate the deck on your property. The first step in this process is to check with your locality's code enforcement office. It's wise to determine the permissible locations and boundaries for your deck before any effort goes into choosing the location.

Checking for Restrictive Covenants

You must also check the deed to your property. There may be restrictions contained in it. These could prevent you from locating your deck on certain portions of your property. In many of the newer subdivisions there are covenants that apply to all the properties within them. If the developer wanted to protect the integrity of his development, more than likely he would use covenants to do so.

It is not uncommon for developers to buy a large tract of land and then develop it in various stages. To develop the whole project at once would require a much larger initial investment. This is not desirable to most developers. Therefore, they improve one section at a time. Because of this, they still have a very large financial interest in the neighborhood after the first phase is completed.

Imagine the consequences if some homeowners, who purchased homes in phase one, made less than desirable "improvements." These could range from painting houses unpleasing colors to raising farm animals. Anything of that nature would have a devastating effect on the developer's ability to continue to sell houses in the development.

What can a developer do to prevent something like this from happening? He can place a restriction on the use of the property. It might read like this: "The purchaser of this property cannot raise chickens, sheep, swine, steer, or any other farm animals on this property." When such a statement is placed on the deed, it becomes a restrictive covenant of that property.

By using certain legal language, the developer can make that covenant remain on the deed and apply to all succeeding buyers. Most developers do so to protect their interests. If your deed contains restrictive covenants of that nature, they will most likely be quite restrictive. Be sure to check your deed for restrictive covenants.

Easements

Your deed may also contain an easement that was granted to another party. A utility company or neighbor may have a deeded right-of-way across your property. If the location of your deck would block that right-of-way, you must make other arrangements, which might include providing a different right-of-way that is satisfactory to the utility or neighbor. If an agreement can't be reached, the deck cannot be placed in the desired location. Because of these instances, and the possibility of others, your deed should be carefully checked before the planning process begins.

Building and Zoning Codes

Building and zoning codes must also be checked beforehand. Otherwise, you risk wasting time planning a location that will not be permitted. The process of choosing a location will then have to start over. All the time and effort spent choosing your first location will have been a waste.

It is possible, however, to appeal the code requirements. A proper understanding of the appeals process will improve your chances of succeeding in your appeal. Nearly every town and city across the country has adopted some form of building and zoning codes. The main purpose for these codes is to protect people from dangerous building practices and to protect the integrity of the community.

The building code sets minimum standards for residential and commercial construction. These standards, when adopted by town or city governments, are a matter of law and must be followed. The code is exhaustive in its completeness. Everything from the stairs that lead to your front door to the design of the tallest of skyscrapers is covered by the building code. It primarily deals with the methods and materials used in construction.

You can expect the building code to regulate the materials and strength of your deck's foundation, and to require minimum sizes and strengths of wood to be used. It will also require minimum nail sizes and minimum heights for railings, and it will contain other regulations of a similar nature. Again, its purpose is to protect the public.

Imagine, if you will, that you live in a town that has not adopted any building code. Let's say that you want a deck built, extending from your second-story bedroom out over a steep hillside. You obtain three estimates and go with the lowest one. Once it is complete, you have a few friends over to admire the view from the deck and it collapses under the weight of the people. Thankfully, this is only an example.

What would cause the tragedy in this example? Without a building code, the builder could use smaller and less expensive wood members. The result would be a deck that's not sufficiently strong enough to hold the heavy loads placed on it occasionally. As illustrated by this example, building codes serve a very useful function and must be taken seriously. One might ask, "If building codes are so necessary and important, should anyone seek relief from them through the appeals process?"

The answer is clearly yes; however, there are some conditions to that yes. I have served for more than five years on a building code appeals board. During this time, I've observed that in the majority of the cases, the appeal was granted only if the applicant could show that an adequate safety margin was maintained.

If you appeal an item in the building code, you must show that your alternative will provide the same level of safety required by the code. I've found most people on these boards to be reasonable in their judgment, and they are willing to help you in any possible way. However, you must be willing to make modifications in your plan that are necessary to ensure a proper margin of safety.

To appeal an item in the building code, inquire about the appeals process at your town's or city's building department. You will be given forms to fill out and return. Once these are returned, your appeal will be scheduled on the agenda for the next meeting. However, before you fill out the forms, talk to several different qualified people to get their suggestions and advice. This will increase your chances of getting your appeal approved.

The first person to talk to is the code enforcement officer or building inspector. He will have a great deal of knowledge about the process. It is well worth your time to ask as many questions as he is willing to answer. Go to him with a humble attitude, stating that you are a novice in this area and need some helpful suggestions. More often than not, he will be happy to assist you.

You may also want to go to one meeting of the appeals board to see what actually takes place. This will give you a quick but valuable education on the appeals process. In so doing, you'll have a better feel for what the members of the board want to see in an appeal in order to approve it. After the meeting, talk to several of the people who appealed and get their perspectives on the process. By doing this type of homework, your chances for a successful appeal are greatly increased.

Zoning Ordinances

On occasion the building code will prevent you from building the deck you want. But far more frequently, the zoning ordinance contains the lethal restrictions that destroy your plan. The building code deals primarily with structural safety; the zoning ordinance deals primarily with aesthetic aspects of construction. The zoning ordinance contains restrictions on lot sizes, building setbacks from property lines, permitted uses of property, traffic impact, lighting, noise, odors, and other similar items.

Zoning ordinances are adopted to protect the public and to preserve the integrity of the community.

Many cities and towns use the zoning ordinance to uphold and ensure a high quality of life in their particular area. As a result, the zoning code is very political in nature and not nearly as straightforward as the building code.

As the building code is appealable, so, too, is the zoning ordinance. I have been a member of a zoning board of appeals for nearly five years. I have seen the difficulty of obtaining an approval for a variance or special exception to the zoning ordinance. It's much more difficult than winning approval of an exception to the building code.

The process of appealing the zoning ordinance is in many ways similar to appealing the building code. The first step is going to the zoning office of your municipality and getting the necessary forms. You should also talk to the code enforcement officer. Take as much of his time as he will give you. Try to glean from him insight into the appeals process in your city or town. Be sure to ask him, in an indirect way, the elements of an appeal on which the board will look most favorably. Make sure you include those in your appeal.

You must also attend at least one zoning board of appeals public hearing. This will give you a better feel for the types of responses the board would like to see. Be sure to do this before you fill out and turn in your application. It will be supplied to each member of the board in advance of the public hearing. Sometimes members of the board will have already determined before the hearing how they will vote because of something contained in the application, although they are not supposed to do that.

Therefore, it's essential that you fill out the application only after you have thoroughly done your homework. The information contained in your application will determine the outcome of your case. Be sure that your completed application is politically acceptable to the zoning board.

In addition to this, before going to the public hearing of your appeal, discuss your intentions with your neighbors. Most cities and towns send notices of your appeal to your abuttors (those whose property adjoins yours) and other interested parties. They have the right to address the board at the public hearing and offer their input. It will be much better for you to speak with them beforehand and win their support.

If they do not agree with your point of view, you will, at the very least, have time to prepare a response to their negative input. You will also have time to speak to those people who do support your appeal and ask for their support at the public hearing. You should try to have your supporters outnumber the people who will be speaking against your appeal. This will increase your chances of success.

In deciding whether or not to appeal the zoning or the building code, consider the alternatives. Is it possible to meet the requirements of the code by modifying your plan? Often a yes answer to that question is reason enough for a zoning board of appeals to deny your request for an exception.

Consider an example. A homeowner wants to build a deck 14 feet wide and 16 feet long. The zoning code will only allow one that is 8 feet by 16 feet. The deck that the homeowner wants can be modified to meet the code simply by making it 6 feet narrower. Why should the zoning board of appeals grant a variance? The homeowner's desire for a larger deck often is not an acceptable reason for the board to approve the request.

Instead of testifying to the board that a larger deck is desired, the homeowner should give the reasons a larger deck is needed. Maybe relatives, who live out of town, often visit for the weekend. An 8 foot by 16 foot deck is not large enough to accommodate both families for the frequent cookouts they have together. This should be stated to the board. It is a much stronger reason for the board to grant the variance.

AESTHETICS AND FUNCTION

After you have determined the permissible locations, according to city regulations, you will be able to decide on a location for your deck. Two major aspects to consider in deciding the location are aesthetics and function. Both must be carefully considered to ensure your deck will suit your needs and add to the attractiveness and value of your home.

At this point, refer to the checklists you have filled out. As you plan the location and the deck itself, be careful to make sure you are fulfilling the objectives laid out in the checklist. The mechanics of putting your ideas on paper in the form of sketches, and then scale drawings, will be discussed later in this chapter.

Accessibility and Traffic Flow

The first element to consider as part of the function of the deck is accessibility. Will its location be conducive to a smooth flow of traffic? You would not want your deck in a location that inhibits ease of use. Using the checklist for help, determine the types of uses and the most likely routes inside your home to get to and from the deck. This will play an important role in the overall design.

As you consider the flow of traffic to and from your deck, make sure you do not limit yourself to existing traffic corridors. Remember that a new door can be installed in any wall. A window can also be replaced by a door. Be sure to consider the changes in traffic flow in your home that will occur because of a new exterior entrance. With careful consideration, an existing smooth traffic flow can be preserved, or minor flaws that are present can be improved or eliminated.

It's best to consider the traffic flow for each expected use separately. A family afternoon barbecue will generate a different flow of traffic than an evening of entertaining several friends. Look at the expected circulation of each. At the barbecue, the children will probably want to play in the yard. Will the location of the deck allow easy access to this play area? Will the deck be located so you can keep a watchful eye on them as you are preparing the meal?

Will the deck be close enough to the kitchen so the trek with an armful of food and supplies will not require the endurance of an Olympic athlete? Consider the work involved in preparing a meal. If your intentions are to use the deck often in this way, then easy access to the kitchen should be incorporated in your plan.

Think also about the cleanup process. Will the location of the deck facilitate an easy cleanup? Will there be an easy route to go from the deck to the place where trash is stored, for example, a garage or shed? You certainly would not want to bring all the trash back into the house to dispose of it.

Another item pertaining to barbecues is a bathroom. The children who were playing in the yard will probably need to wash their hands before sitting down to eat. Will the deck's location have easy access to a bathroom? It is a good idea to plan for easy bathroom access no matter what types of uses you are planning for your deck.

Contrast the above traffic circulation with the traffic flow that would occur at an evening of outdoor entertaining. Unless you have a very well-lit yard, and your friends enjoy outdoor sports, you will not require access to the yard at night. Neither will you require access to the trash storage area.

Instead, traffic will be flowing from the place where your guests park their cars. Will you want them to go to the front entrance of your home and flow through it? Would you like the deck to be located so guests may come and go without creating traffic through the house?

During this time of entertaining and socializing, some guests may get chilly as the night air cools off. They may want to go inside for a while to warm up. Will there be a room just inside to accommodate them? You will probably serve food and drinks to your guests. Is the deck located close to the great room or living room where guests can sit and enjoy refreshments? Maybe you have a wet bar where they can be served. If so, will the location of the deck allow for a smooth flow of traffic from the deck to the wet bar?

As in these two examples, choosing the right location involves determining the types of uses and their associated traffic flows. It's almost impossible to place your deck in a location that's ideal for every type of function. Give a considerable amount of thought to your own particular situation before deciding on the location of your deck. By doing this, the deck will likely be in an ideal location for the types of functions you'll be using it for most.

The checklists in the Appendix have been compiled with the intent of helping you complete a thorough analysis of your deck needs. It's not possible for them to contain all the information and questions necessary for a complete analysis of every circumstance. Nevertheless, once you have filled them out, they will give you a very detailed summary of the information needed to formulate your deck plan.

Deciding on a Location

You may find that you are having trouble deciding between two or more locations for your deck. A suggested way to determine the ideal location is to make several photocopies of the completed checklists. Consider each possible location individually. Go through the checklist for each location, checking off in the space provided all the desires fulfilled.

Notice on Checklist #6 there is a space provided to rate each desire on a scale of 1 to 10 according to importance. Once you have completed the checklists for each location, add all the scores and compare the totals. Seldom do the scores come extremely close together. Usually, there is one that is much higher than the others. This is a strong indication that this site is preferable to any of the alternatives.

NATURAL CONDITIONS

Another factor to consider in determining location is natural conditions existing on and below the ground. Nearly any obstacle can be overcome. If there is a high outcropping or ledge, it can be removed by blasting. If there is a low boggy area, it can be filled. If there is a deep layer of clay, it can be dug through to install the foundation. However, some of these ways of overcoming obstacles can be quite expensive. Unless you are operating on an unlimited budget, the cost of removing a natural obstacle will weigh heavily in your choice of locations.

The weather and climate will also have an effect on your deck location. So, too, will the area of the country in which you live. The temperature can vary by as much as 30° F from one side of a building to another. If your home is located in the desert southwest, you will certainly not want to place your deck on the hottest side of the house. Likewise, if your home is in a cold northern state, you will not want to place your deck in the coldest area of your yard.

You must determine the microclimate for each side of your home. How much sunshine an area receives is the most important factor that determines the microclimate. In general, the northern side of your home will be the coolest because it receives the least amount of sun. East facing decks usually are the warmest in the morning, but coolest in the afternoon and evening. This occurs because late in morning they are out of the sun's direct rays, and they remain in the shade for the rest of the day.

However, these are just generalities. A large tree on the east side of your home could shade that entire side of your property. It would eliminate any direct morning sun. If that were the case, the southern side would likely be the warmest in the morning. The west side is usually the hottest, because it receives direct sunshine from shortly after noon until sunset. Again, this is a generality and there are many factors that could alter the effects of nature in your particular case.

In addition to sunshine, you need to consider the other elements of weather and how they may affect the location of your deck. If you live in an area that experiences frequent summer showers, you may want to locate your deck close to your house. By doing so, it will enable you to extend the house roof, providing shelter for you to remain outside during these warm-weather showers.

If your area experiences a large amount of precipitation annually, you will need to take extra precautions. Try to protect your deck from rapid deterioration caused by the weather. One possible solution would be a roof extension to prevent most of the rain and snow from falling on the deck. You could also install a gutter and downspout system, or use higher grade materials that will stand up to the elements much better than standard materials. You may also allocate extra dollars to treat your deck regularly with preservatives, or choose some combination of the above.

If you live in an area of the country that experiences winter snowfalls, you will need to take extra measures to protect your deck from winter damage. Snow and ice sliding off a roof can crush benches, snap railings, or even collapse the whole deck in extreme cases. The type of protective measure you take will depend on your own situation.

Carefully examine your home's design. Knowledge of the winter conditions in your area and proper planning will prevent any midwinter mishaps from occurring. Make sure that railings and benches are located away from places where snow and ice are likely to fall from the roof. Try not to locate your deck in an area where a large volume of snow comes off the roof regularly. If a deck must be located in such an area, plan on building it stronger than is required by the building code.

Wind must also be considered in the planning process. Depending on personal preference and the area of the country you live in, you may want to have a breeze blowing across your deck. There are three kinds of wind: occasional high speed winds generated by a storm, seasonal prevailing winds, and very localized daily breezes. Knowing the types of wind that affect your property, and when they are prevalent, will allow you to take advantage of, or minimize, their effects.

If you have not lived in your area long enough to know the typical wind conditions that exist, talk to a neighbor who has. Once you have determined the normal wind directions, you can plan your deck accordingly. You may decide that a barrier is needed to shield the wind. Typical choices include a solid fence, dense shrubbery, or a broken fence, such as one with boards spaced a few inches apart.

These same materials could be used to achieve the opposite effect: increasing the wind flow across your deck. If you live in an area of the country that is very warm, you may want to use any breezes for the increased comfort of their cooling effect. Instead of using the fence as a barrier, locate it in such a way that it funnels the breeze right across your deck. Again, a proper knowledge of the prevalent winds and careful planning will allow you to achieve the desired results.

Referring back to the checklist, you will see the questions about the different microclimates existing on your property. Spend the necessary time evaluating these to ensure accurate information on your checklist. The temptation is to guess, without putting any effort into studying the differences between one side and another. I caution you against doing that. If you have been in your home for a decade or longer, you may have a good enough feel for the different microclimates that exist to guess accurately. However, upon further inspection and research, you will probably uncover some facts that you were not aware of.

DECK STYLE

Another element to consider in the planning process is eye appeal. An unattractive deck that will accommodate all your functions will be much less enjoyable than one that meets your needs and is very attractive. Alluring and appealing decks do not just happen. They are planned that way. There are four different kinds of decks: low-level, multi-level, high-level, and roof decks (see Figures 2 through 5).

Choosing the right deck for your property will enhance its attractiveness. Choosing the wrong one will give your deck an undesirable appearance. If you have a ranch style home, it would be an error to choose a high-level deck. Likewise, if you have a very tall home, choosing a very low-level deck will not increase the attractiveness of your property.

Not only the type of deck but the other elements of deck design must work together to create unity. The shape, location, types of materials used, railing and bench style, and pattern on the deck floor must all look as though they belong together. If any one component appears out of place, the whole project will lose much of its charm.

The goal is to make the whole deck blend with the architectural style of the house and yard. If your home is a formal Victorian style, you would not want a rustic deck. The deck's design should match the style of the house and complement its appearance to create a very inviting look.

Another element to consider is proportion. Your deck should be large enough to accommodate your functions but not so large that it overwhelms your

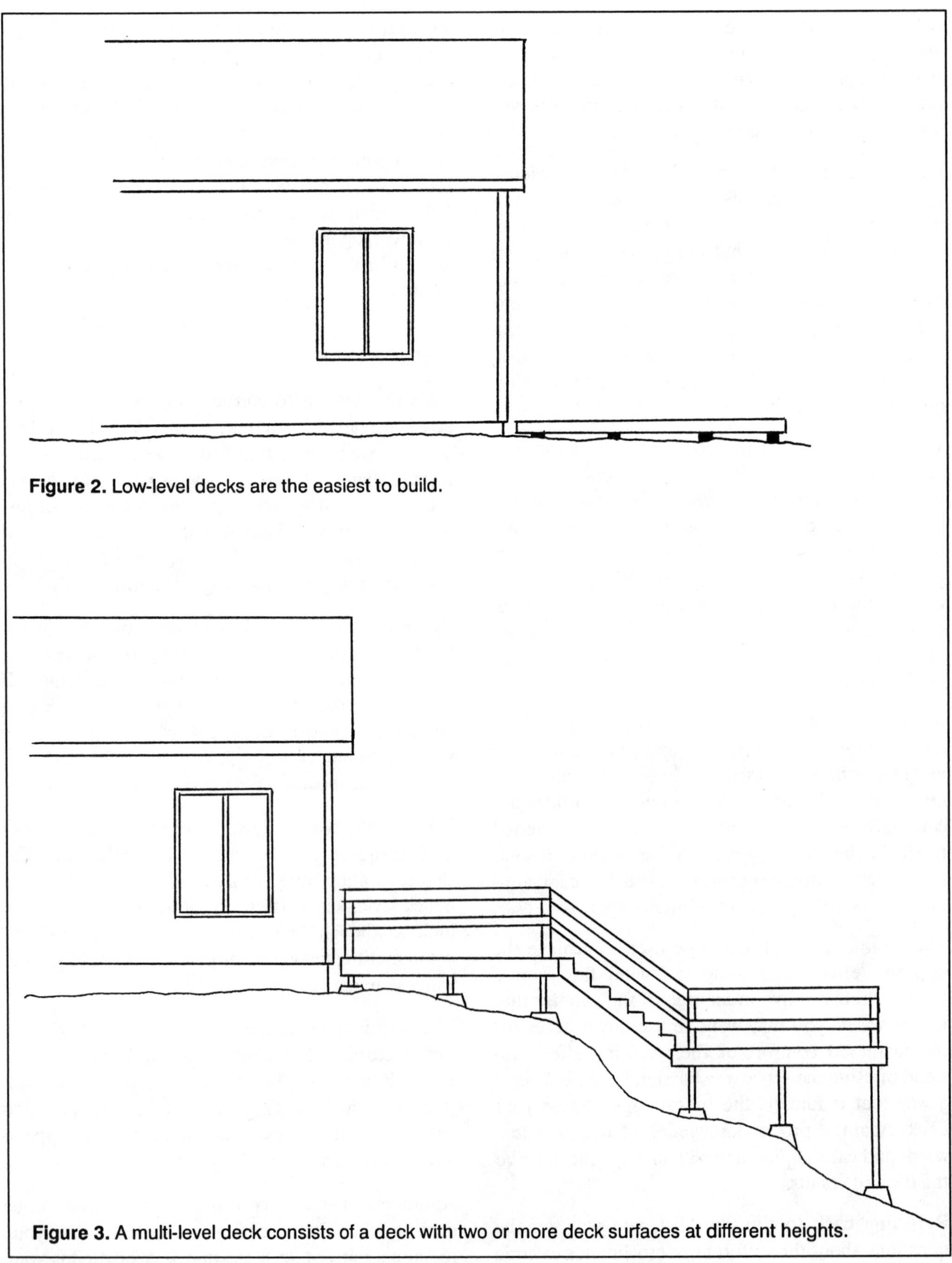

Figure 2. Low-level decks are the easiest to build.

Figure 3. A multi-level deck consists of a deck with two or more deck surfaces at different heights.

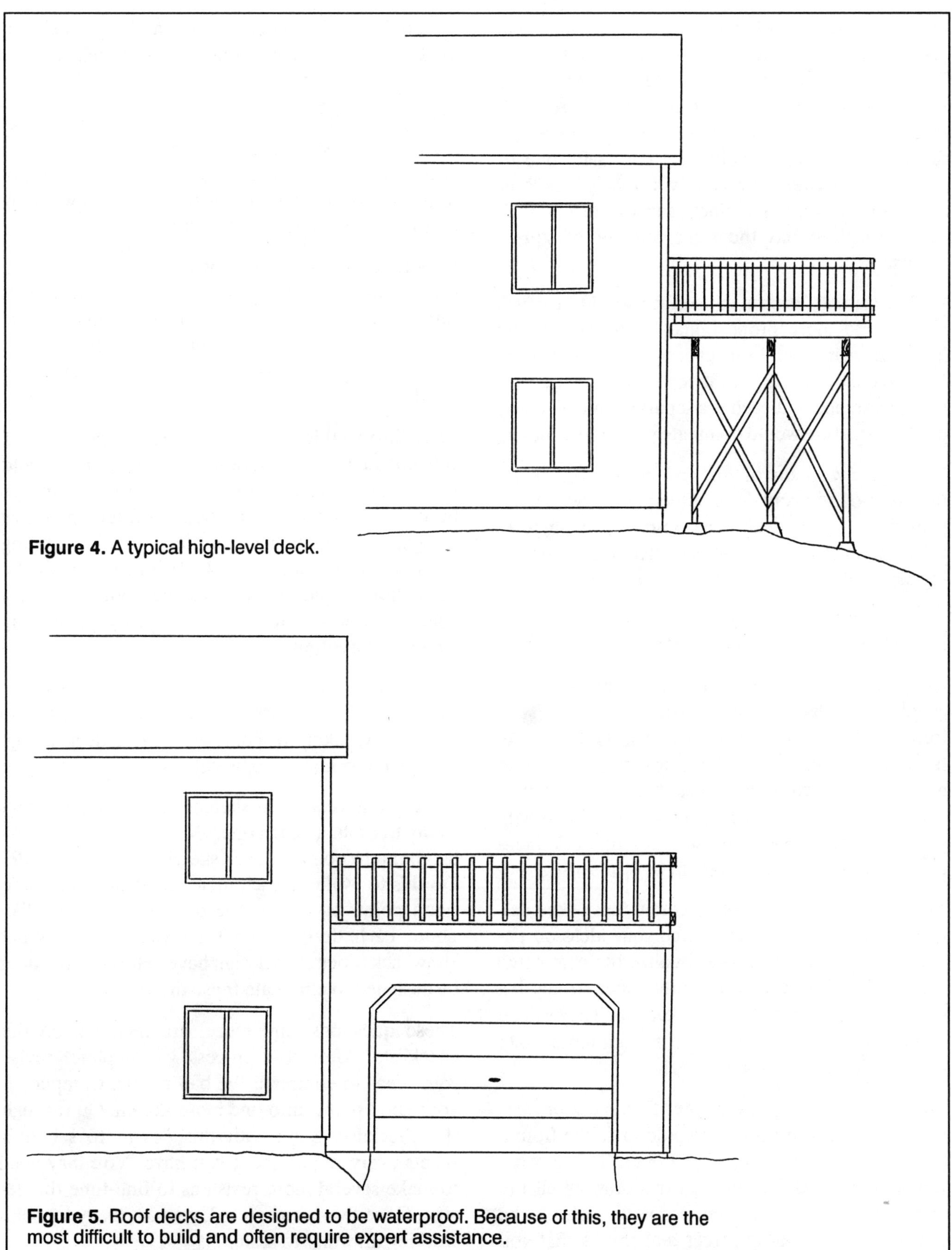

Figure 4. A typical high-level deck.

Figure 5. Roof decks are designed to be waterproof. Because of this, they are the most difficult to build and often require expert assistance.

entire property. Neither should it be so small that just a few pieces of furniture give it a crowded feeling. If you have a small home but would like a large deck, try to avoid building one large deck surface. A better design divides the square footage into two deck surfaces. By planning a multi-level deck with one or more steps between levels, it will not look as large and overpowering as a single surface deck would, even though it has the same amount of square footage.

In this example, each deck surface would be much smaller and more proportional to the size of the house. By using a multi-level design, each half of the deck would be on a different horizontal plane, giving the appearance that each is a separate unit. This way neither structure would dominate your yard or home.

It's a wise investment of time and energy to give careful attention to every detail affecting the overall appearance of your deck. The hours spent on forethought and planning for an eye-catching and appealing deck will yield years of pleasure and enjoyment.

PUTTING IDEAS ON PAPER

After you have completed all the checklists and decided on the deck's location, you will need to start forming ideas of what your deck will look like. As these ideas come to mind, it's best to put them on paper in the form of rough sketches. At first they need not be to scale. Their purpose is only to help you visualize different possibilities of deck ideas and show you how they might fit in your setting.

You need not be an artist to draw these sketches. Obviously, the better you sketch your ideas on paper, the easier it will be to visualize the completed deck. Even if your artistic ability is not strong, it's important for you to do these sketches. They will be building blocks for later use in making more exact working drawings to scale.

The best sketch to put on paper first is a *plan view*. Imagine what your property would look like from a bird's perspective above your house. This is what you should sketch. Include on this drawing all the important features of your property such as the driveway, any walkways, trees and shrubs that you would like to keep, steep slopes, and any other item that exists. A sample of this type of sketch is shown in Figure 6.

You should also include the location of any easements that exist on your property. Once this sketch is completed, make fifteen or more photocopies of it. Again, this drawing is not to scale. You will only be using it to visualize different ideas.

Now that you have this to work on, start outlining the various ideas that you have for your deck. It is important to record all your ideas. Although some may not seem very good, don't throw them away. You will be able to use the bad ones as well as the good ones.

Take time to think about the different possibilities. It is not advisable to sit down on one afternoon and do all these sketches. Allow yourself some time to be creative and to think about different potential designs. Be thinking about them in the morning when you're driving to work, at lunchtime, on the drive home, and in the evening. When an idea comes to you, be sure to sketch it on your drawing so it isn't forgotten.

Do this for several days, or until you feel that you've exhausted all the possibilities. By doing so, you're much more likely to come up with a deck design that you'll be really happy with.

Once you have all your sketches complete, it is necessary to evaluate each one. Go through your checklists point by point for each sketch that you've made. Do this to evaluate each idea and glean from it the good points as well as the bad. What do you like about each design? What do you dislike? What drawbacks does each design have? How can the deck be designed to eliminate these drawbacks?

These questions, and more, are included on the checklists. After this process is complete, revise your ideas to eliminate the bad points. Compile all your good points into one more sketch. Go through the checklists again with this design to see if it meets every requirement you have. You may need to make several more revisions to fine-tune the design. Once this is completed, you are ready to make working drawings to scale.

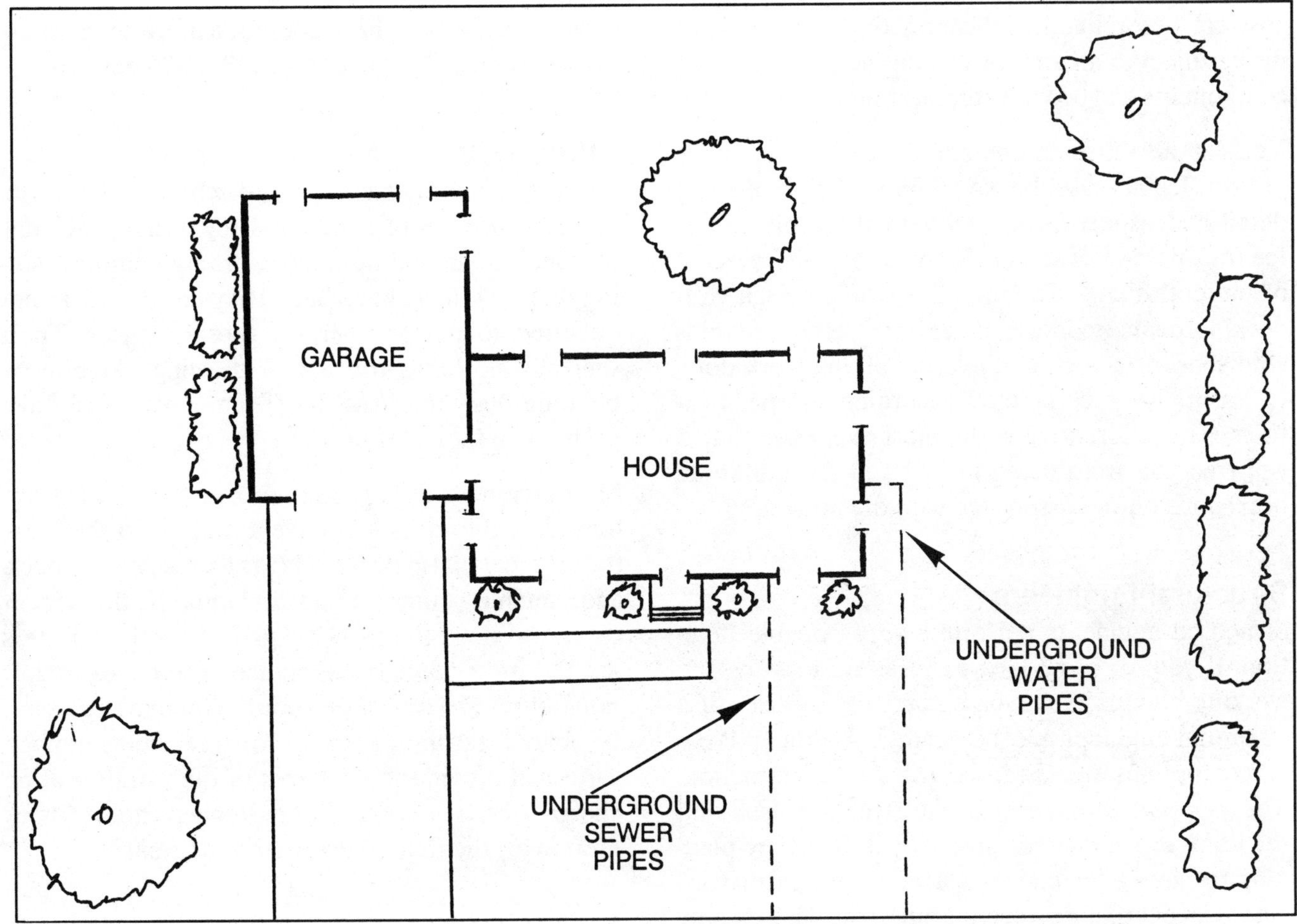

Figure 6. Plan view of property should show all the important features to consider in planning your deck.

SUBCONTRACTORS

You may decide that you are not qualified to create your working drawings. If so, you'll need to hire a professional to complete them for you. It's essential to know the different types of professionals available in the marketplace and the aspects of your deck project with which they can help. This will aid you in choosing the right one to handle your job. Among the specialists to consider are: architects, structural engineers, building designers, drafters, general contractors, builders, carpenters, brick masons or stonemasons, foundation contractors, excavation contractors, plumbers, electricians, painters, soil scientists or engineers, and landscape architects or designers.

Architects

Architects are licensed professionals with at least a bachelor's degree in architecture. They have been trained to be knowledgeable in all aspects of construction. You can hire an architect in one of several ways: as a consultant, as a subcontractor, to provide you with one or more services, or you can retain one to handle the entire project.

If you hire an architect as a consultant, you can expect to pay between $40 and $75 per hour. He will give advice on any element of your project that you desire, though he may prove particularly valuable for suggesting ideas to improve your design.

If you decide to hire an architect to provide one or more components of your deck project, you may be charged either a flat fee or an hourly rate. It is common for architects to be hired only to design the deck and provide working blueprints. If you choose to do this, fill out the checklists before contacting the architect. He will ask many of the same questions anyway, and it will save time to know the answers beforehand. Subcontracting part of your deck project to an architect means all the remaining components will be your responsibility.

You can also hire an architect to handle the entire project. In this case, he would be in charge of every detail and aspect associated with the project. The fee for this type of service is usually 10 to 15 percent of the entire cost. The architect would design your deck, provide working blueprints, negotiate bids with subcontractors, and oversee all the work done to ensure it is completed according to specifications. This alternative is the most expensive, but it will free you from being involved in the multitude of responsibilities associated with the project.

Structural Engineers

Structural engineers perform a very valuable function. If you, or someone you hire, are drawing the working blueprints, at some point the services of a structural engineer may be needed. A structural engineer designs the essential parts of construction. They support the weight of the structure itself and the items expected to be placed on it. If you are planning to have a cantilevered deck (a design that includes an overhang projecting out), you will probably want a structural engineer to design that part of it.

Structural engineers are held legally responsible for the work that they do. If their design fails, they will be held liable. You can be sure their designs are safe. Their fees generally range from $30 to $60 per hour, although in some instances you can get their services for free. If your deck requires one or more steel I-beams, try to find a structural steel company that has an engineer on staff. Many do. If you buy the steel from one of those companies, the company will usually provide the engineering work for free. Just specify what you need the steel for, and an engineer will perform all the calculations at no charge.

Building Designers

Building designers in general have much of the same training that architects have, but haven't spent as much time and money on continuing education. A building designer does not have an architect's license. Because of this, they can provide many of the same services that an architect does for a more economical price. Fees usually range from $18 to $35 per hour.

Drafters

Drafters primarily have gone to school to learn the technical aspects of drawing. They usually have not had the design, mathematical, or engineering training that architects have had. They are therefore not qualified to perform any of those services. Their specialty is doing the actual drawing. Architects, building designers, and large lumberyards all have drafters on their staff.

Most architects do not do their own drawings. They formulate the ideas and have a drafter do the illustrations. If you use the checklists to design your deck and sketch it yourself, a drafter would be the person to hire to draw the working plans to scale. Drafters are the most economical choice. Their fees usually range from $10 to $20 per hour. You may, however, be able to get their services for free. Many lumberyards will provide the services of their drafter at no charge if you purchase your lumber there. Check around for such a lumberyard in your area.

General Contractors

General contractors can provide all the services necessary to complete your deck job once you have a set of blueprints. They will do the work themselves or hire subcontractors to do it for them. If you provide a copy of the plans, they will give you a quote for the entire job. Some states require the licensing of general contractors. Others do not. Make sure you thoroughly check the background of any general contractor before you hire him.

During prosperous economic times, employees of general contractors who are merely laborers quit their jobs and go into business for themselves. This is particularly true in states that do not require one to have a license to be a general contractor. Being new in the field, and many times not qualified, these inexperienced people are a risky choice. Many, many problems arise on jobs where the general contractor lacks experience or is incompetent. It's best to hire a knowledgeable and experienced person to run your job.

Builders

Builders are quite similar to general contractors, except they are more likely to have employees on their crew to do the actual labor. Most of what applies to general contractors applies to builders as well. Knowledge, experience, and quality of craftsmanship vary greatly among builders. It is important to check out any builder or building company thoroughly before you hire him or them.

Carpenters

Carpenters primarily specialize in building or repairing wooden structures. If you need a person with building skills to assist you in building your deck, shop around for a good carpenter. Carpenters have much specialized knowledge of building materials and construction techniques.

Brick Masons and Stonemasons

Your plans may include masonry elements. If you want a barbecue pit, a brick walkway, or a stone retaining wall, you will probably need the services of a brick or stone mason. Unless you have done this type of work before, don't attempt it without the help of a professional. If you've ever watched one of these tradesmen work, you've seen how easy it looks to do. It definitely isn't. It requires lots of schooling and practice to become good at it. It also requires expensive tools to do a proper job. It could cost more in the long run than any money you might save trying to do the job yourself. Let the experts handle it.

Foundation Contractors

The building of a foundation is another very specialized trade. Depending upon the complexity of your foundation design, you may need a foundation contractor. It's easy for one to cut corners that a homeowner will not discover. Make sure that you are hiring a reputable person to do the job. Shop around and try to get one who will give you a written guarantee against cracks developing for one or two years. If cracks don't develop within this time frame, they usually won't develop at all.

Excavation Contractors

You may also need to hire an excavation contractor. You might need one to change the grading of your yard or to dig holes for a foundation. Your deck plan may include elimination of a few trees. You would need an excavation contractor to remove the stumps. Excavation contractors' services vary greatly in price. A small company with only two or three pieces of equipment will likely give you the best price. Many machines cost over $100,000 new. If you call a larger company with a dozen or more of these, their price will be higher because of their large overhead. Shop around and only hire a big company if your job demands it.

Plumbers

You may desire an additional exterior faucet near your deck. You may even want a fountain centered in your deck. Depending on the complexity of the job, and the amount of experience that you have, it is possible to do this type of work yourself. You can get by with a few relatively inexpensive tools if your task is a simple one. If you're not certain you can handle the job, it's best to call a plumber.

Electricians

You may also need the services of an electrician. I recommend that you hire one if you need any electrical work done at all. If a mistake is made doing plumbing, you may get wet; if you make a mistake doing electrical work, you may get electrocuted. If you would like to add a couple of outlets, the electrician can tell you if they can be added to an existing circuit. A new circuit may need to be added. If your deck project includes many new lights and outlets, your electrician will know if your service entrance can handle the additional load placed on it. Your service may need to be upgraded.

Painters

Many homeowners paint their projects themselves. Painting requires few tools (a couple of paint brushes and rollers) and very little experience. However, the services of a painter may be desired. Most experienced painters know the good products and which ones to avoid. They will know the best product to use on your project. The range of quality from product to product is very large. Most paint salesmen proclaim their product to be top of the line and state that it will last for many years. However, they are paid to sell the product, so it is in their best interest to tell you that. A painter can give you information based on experience.

Soil Scientists and Engineers

Your property may have difficult ground conditions. Elements such as a steep slope or soft ground, caused by certain types of soil, may exist. If so, you may need the services of a soil scientist or soil engineer. Depending on the size and scope of your project, he would evaluate the soil conditions of your site and recommend design modifications to your foundation. If your project is large, he would forward information to a structural engineer who would design the foundation.

If you are uncertain about the need for such services, it's best to call a soil scientist for an initial evaluation. The cost is relatively low, usually around $75. He will take soil samples from different locations on your property using an auger. You will receive an immediate analysis. After this initial consultation, you'll know whether your soil will support a normal foundation. If it will not, you'll have a good idea of the types of modifications that will be required.

Landscape Designers and Architects

You may also choose to hire a landscape architect or designer. Landscape designers may have much of the same education that a landscape architect has, but they don't have the architect's license. It is possible in some states to start a landscape company without any formal education in the field at all. A person could hang a sign out, hire one or two laborers, and call himself a landscape design and contracting company. Because this is not only possible but frequently happens, you must be careful whom you hire.

The more time you spend checking a person's or a company's background before you hire, the more likely you are to hire a good one. It's essential to talk to other people who have had work done by the contractor. Look at the work he has done. Is the quality of work satisfactory? Ask the homeowner questions about the contractor. Was the contractor helpful and cooperative? Was the contractor punctual? Was the job organized and performed in a professional manner? What didn't you like about the job or the contractor? Would you recommend this company?

Get estimates from at least three contractors you have found to be reliable. Make sure they are all given the same job description, containing enough information for them to give you an accurate quote. It's wise to tell them you are getting other estimates. In so doing, you'll let them know that you're not a naive homeowner, and it will also put pressure on them to give you their best price.

If all other things are equal, go with the one who gives you the best price. Before you sign a contract, it's important to verify that the contractor has the required insurance. Ask for copies of his insurance policy. If employees are involved, make sure they are covered by worker's compensation. You should also verify his insurance for property damage and public liability.

Make sure that any contractor you plan on hiring is financially solvent. Check bank and credit references. You don't want your contractor to go out of business in the middle of your job. Once this is completed, you are ready to prepare a contract. It's unwise to sign a contract that has been prepared by the contractor without your involvement. His interest is in protecting himself; his contract will reflect that. There will probably be very little in it to protect you. It's best for you to have an active part in preparing a sound contract.

CONTRACTS

The contract should include the working blueprints, detailed descriptions of all materials, and a time schedule for the project. It should also include a detailed description of the work to be performed, the method of payment, penalties for failure to perform, a provision for lien waiver, and written guarantees on materials and workmanship.

A complete set of working blueprints should be made part of the contract. They should illustrate, in detail, what the completed deck will look like. Do not leave any aspect of the deck or its construction undecided when you sign the contract. If necessary, delay the signing of the contract until all the specific details can be included.

The contract should also contain detailed descriptions of all materials to be used. This includes brand name, model numbers if any, grades and species of lumber, and strengths of concrete used in the foundation. If any of these are left out, the contractor may use the least expensive and lowest quality materials available.

It is important to agree on a time schedule with any person you hire. Be sure to include this in the contract. Do not accept verbal promises. Insist that they be in writing. As the work is being done, there are many reasons for delays to develop. It's common for them to occur. Most contractors are familiar with the types of events that cause delays and will factor them into the estimated time to complete the project.

It is very important to list specifically and give detailed descriptions of all the work that you expect the contractor to perform. If you expect a daily cleanup of the yard where work was done, list that in the contract. If you expect the contractor to prepare the site by removing fences or shrubs, list that also. Be sure to include in the contract all the tasks you want the contractor to complete. Avoid generalities that cover substantial amounts of work in just a sentence. They leave too much room for confusion. Be meticulous in describing the work to be done. Remember, if it is not included in the contract, the contractor is not obligated to do it.

The contract must also specify the method of payment. Typically, a percentage is given at the signing of the contract. This gives the contractor funds to purchase part of the materials. On smaller jobs the payment arrangement may be 50% upon signing of the contract and 50% upon completion of the work. On larger jobs there are more than two installments. Payment is divided into several parts, and funds are dispersed as the job is completed. It is important not to give the final payment until all the work is completed.

You may also want to include penalties in your contract. A typical penalty is a fine for every day after the projected completion date that the project runs. This is usually only seen in larger commercial jobs, but it may be desirable to include penalties in your contract. If they are included, they make a good incentive for the contractor to place a higher priority on your job. The absence of such penalties means the contractor could delay your job for any reason without suffering any damages.

You should also include a provision for a lien waiver. If you hire a general contractor who will be hiring subcontractors, you'll want to be sure they are paid accordingly. Make a provision in the contract for him to provide to you signed statements by the subcontractors who worked on the project. These should state that they have been paid, and that they give up the right to place a lien on your property for non-payment.

Another important element of the contract is written guarantees. Many states have laws determining the length of time that construction work must be guaranteed. Nevertheless, it's still good to get written guarantees. Whatever the contractor promises you verbally, have it recorded in the contract. Beware of trusting someone because he is friendly and appears to be honest.

POINTS TO REMEMBER

- ❑ Determine *why* you want a deck. Then it will be a simple matter to specify your particular needs.
- ❑ In deciding where to locate the deck, check for restrictive covenants, easements, building codes, and zoning ordinances.
- ❑ Accessibility and traffic flow are important considerations in locating the site for a deck.
- ❑ Natural conditions, such as weather, climate, soil type, and microclimates, must be taken into account.
- ❑ Choose your deck's style for eye appeal and its ability to complement the design of your home.
- ❑ Make sketches of proposed designs and ideas for your deck.
- ❑ Consider hiring an architect, a structural engineer, a building designer, a drafter, or a general contractor to help you prepare a deck design.

2
Drawing Plans to Scale

Trying to draw deck plans without the proper tools will lead to a lot of frustration and a less-than-professional result. However, don't worry. The few tools you do need are inexpensive.

TOOLS

Drawing Board

You'll need a drawing board, but there is no need to purchase a deluxe one at the local art supply store. A sanded piece of plywood about 30" x 36" will do. Alternatives include a wide shelf or a large cutting board. Make sure the edges of your board are straight and smooth, and the angles at the corners are exactly 90°.

It is nice to have a drawing surface that slants. This alleviates neck strain caused by continually looking down. By propping the back of your drawing board up, you will be looking at your work at a more natural angle. If you are using a piece of plywood as a drawing board, you can nail blocking on the back of it to make it slant. Telephone books or thick catalogs could also be used to prop up the back of your board.

T-Square

If you do not already have one, you will need to purchase a T-square (see Figure 8). They come in various lengths, styles, and prices. You need not purchase a deluxe model; the basic tool, which is moderately priced, is all you will need. The T-square slides along the edge of your drawing board, enabling you to draw parallel lines accurately and efficiently.

Triangles

Of equal importance with the T-square, and used in conjunction with it, are the triangles. They come in several different sizes, and are usually made of clear plastic. You'll need two triangles: one that has 45° angles, and one that has 30° and 60° angles (see Figure 9). The best size to get is the 8 inch. If you buy triangles that are calibrated on the sides, you will save time, as you can draw and measure at the same time.

Architect's Scale

An architect's scale (Figure 10) is three-sided, and each surface has its own use. Each side is divided into different proportions indicating 1/8, 1/4, 3/8, 1/2, 3/4, 1.5, and 3 inches to the foot. They are usually "open divided," which means that the units are shown along the entire length of a side. Only the end unit is divided into inches and fractions.

Paper

You can get ordinary drawing paper in rolls or sheets. Any kind of paper that is heavy enough to take a nice line, and will allow you to erase without chewing up the paper, is sufficient.

For your convenience, graph paper is provided on the next page. Photocopy and use it as needed.

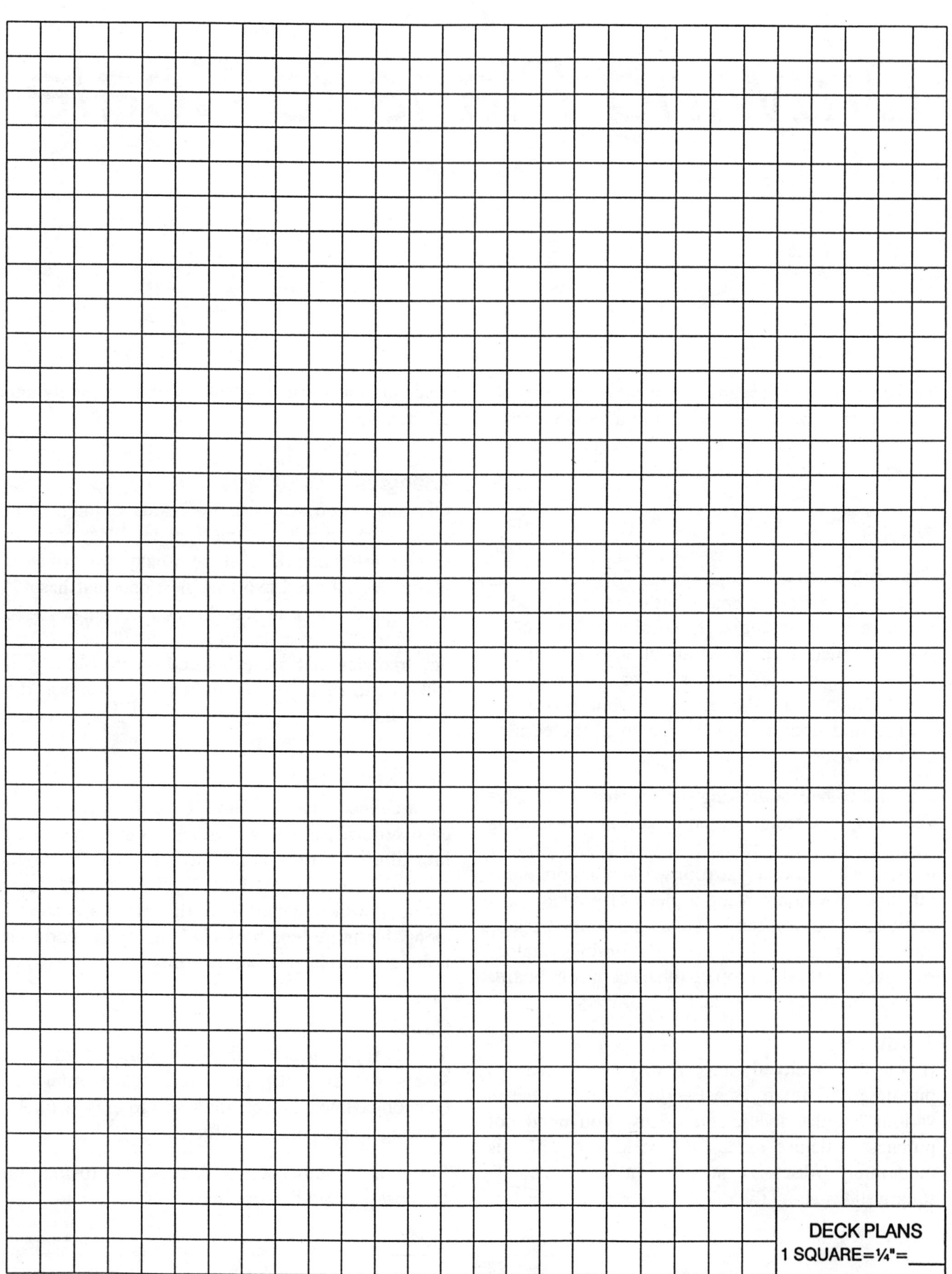
DECK PLANS
1 SQUARE=¼"=____

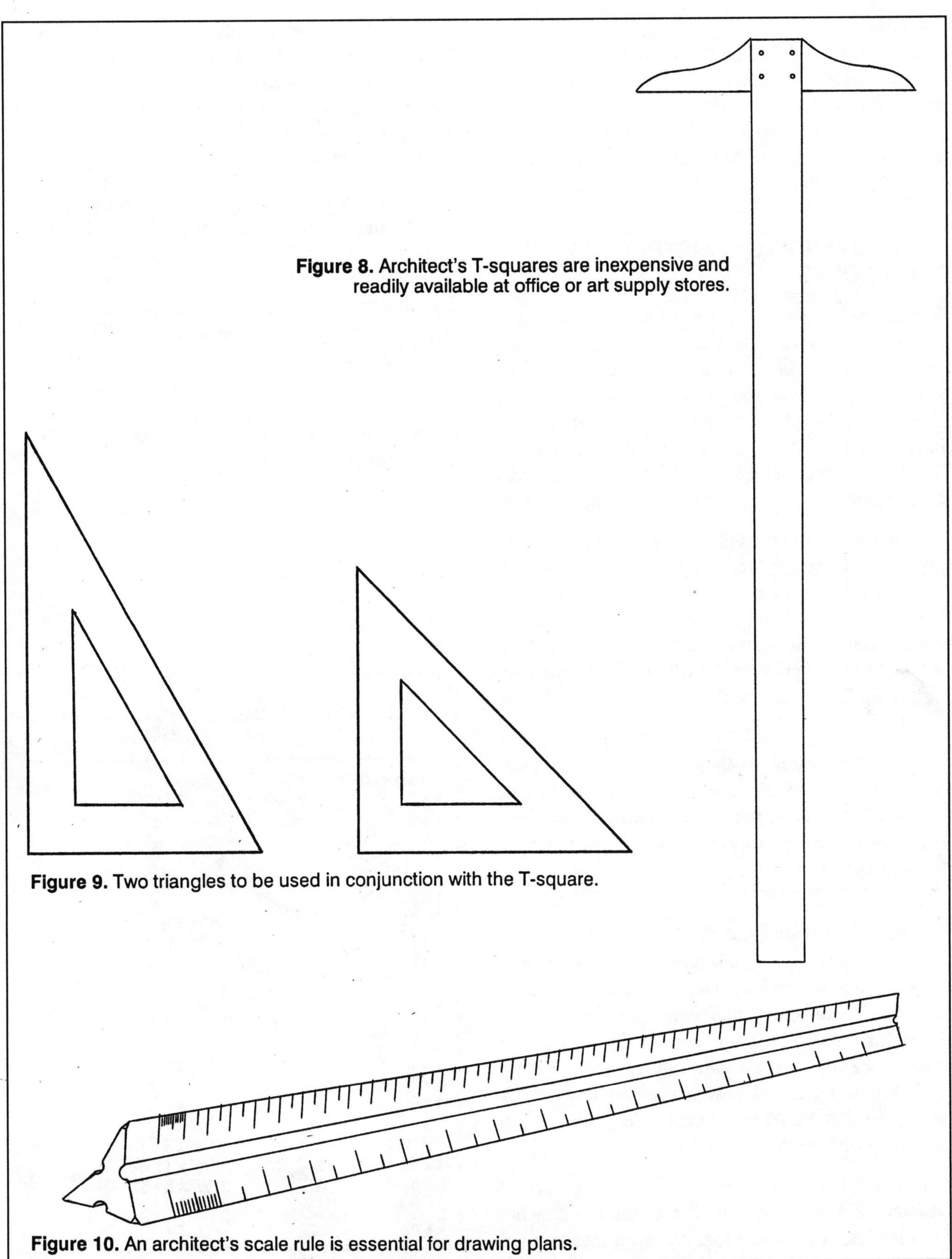

Figure 8. Architect's T-squares are inexpensive and readily available at office or art supply stores.

Figure 9. Two triangles to be used in conjunction with the T-square.

Figure 10. An architect's scale rule is essential for drawing plans.

Pencils

Each drawing will first be done in pencil. Only after it is completed will you use ink. Pencils are graded according to hardness. The scale ranges from 6B, which is very soft, to 9H, which is very hard. You will need only a 2H or 4H, depending on the heaviness of your hand.

UNDERSTANDING CONSTRUCTION TECHNIQUES

Because working scale drawings contain exact specifications of how your deck is to be built, it is important to understand construction techniques before you attempt to draw the plans. Once your plans are finished, they will be a complete set of instructions to build your deck. As such, they must illustrate correct construction techniques, and they must ensure that all elements of the deck will meet building codes.

The following tables will help you determine the proper sizes, spans, and spacings for your deck's structural members. Keep in mind as you use them that they were developed using the BOCA (Building Officials Code Administration) code. Use them to plan and design your deck, but check with your local building department as well. Your local code may be more stringent.

The numbers listed in these tables are maximum limits. You can always choose larger joists, beams, or posts, or you can use closer spacings than those listed. However, you cannot go beyond the limits set forth in these tables.

Table 1: Lumber Sizes

When designing the structural elements of your deck, a crucial bit of knowledge is the difference between *nominal* and *actual* dimensions of lumber. Take, for instance, a 2 x 4. You would think that it measures 2" by 4". It actually only measures 1½" by 3½". When it was first sawn at the mill, it originally measured 2" x 4". At that time it was green (full of sap and moisture) lumber.

When wood dries, it shrinks. Thus after the 2 x 4 has been kiln-dried, it is no longer the full 2 inches by 4 inches. Also, when logs are sawn into lumber, the boards are quite rough and full of splintered edges. They must be planed to be made smooth. Once a board goes through this process it is said to be "dressed" or "surfaced." This process makes a dry board, which has shrunk, even smaller. Thus the actual size is different from the nominal size.

Use this table to determine the actual sizes of the boards and beams listed in the other tables. Beams need not be one solid board. They can be several boards nailed or bolted together. However, when building beams in this way, you must make sure that the built-up beam will be as large as a solid one would be. Say, for example, that your deck design calls for a 6 x 8 beam. You could not fasten three 2 x 8s together as a substitute. The finished product would only be 4½" by 7¼", whereas a solid 6 x 8 would measure 5½" by 7¼".

Table 1
STANDARD DIMENSIONS OF DRIED AND SURFACED LUMBER

Nominal Size	Actual Size
1 x 2	¾" x 1 ½"
1 x 3	¾" x 2 ½"
1 x 4	¾" x 3 ½"
1 x 5	¾" x 4 ½"
1 x 6	¾" x 5 ½"
1 x 8	¾" x 7 ¼"
1 x 10	¾" x 9 ¼"
1 x 12	¾" x 11 ¼"
2 x 3	1 ½" x 2 ½"
2 x 4	1 ½" x 3 ½"
2 x 6	1 ½" x 5 ½"
2 x 8	1 ½" x 7 ¼"
2 x 10	1 ½" x 9 ¼"
2 x 12	1 ½" x 11 ¼"
4 x 4	3 ½" x 3 ½"
4 x 6	3 ½" x 5 ½"
4 x 8	3 ½" x 7 ¼"
4 x 10	3 ½" x 9 ¼"
4 x 12	3 ½" x 11 ¼"
6 x 6	5 ½" x 5 ½"
6 x 8	5 ½" x 7 ¼"
8 x 8	7 ¼" x 7 ¼"

Table 2: Strength Groupings of Common Wood Species

As you will learn in Chapter 3, there are many kinds of wood to choose from for your deck. Each species has a different level of strength. Laboratories have tested these species and graded them according to tensile strength, stiffness, and ability to withstand compression. Though no two species have identical strength, they are classified into three groupings: A, B, and C, with those in group "A" being the strongest, down to those in group "C", which are the least strong. If your choice of wood changes after the working plans for the deck have been made, be sure that the new wood selection is as strong as your original choice.

Table 2
STRENGTH GROUPINGS OF COMMON SOFTWOODS
(Based on #2 and Better Lumber)

Group A: Cypress, Douglas Fir, West Coast Hemlock, Western Larch, Southern Yellow Pine

Group B: Western Red Cedar, White Fir, Eastern Hemlock, Lodgepole Pine, Norway Pine, Ponderosa Pine, Sugar Pine, Northern White Pine, Redwood (clear all heart), Eastern Spruce, Sitka Spruce

Group C: Northern White Cedar, Southern White Cedar, Balsam Fir, Redwood (construction heart or better)

Table 3: Maximum Decking Spans

Decking refers to the boards of a deck's surface that lie on top of the joists. In some designs, joists are not used, and the decking lies directly on the beams. This table will show you the maximum spacing between joists or beams that different size boards can span. Keep in mind that when decks are designed using the maximum allowable spans, they tend to feel a bit springy. For a more solid feel underfoot, use spans that are less than the maximum allowed.

Table 3
MAXIMUM DECKING SPANS

	Species Group		
	A	B	C
Nominal 1" boards laid flat	16"	14"	12"
Pressure-treated 1 1/4" boards laid flat	24"	16"	—
Nominal 2" boards laid flat	30"	24"	20"
Nominal 2 x 3s laid on edge	48"	40"	32"
Nominal 2 x 4s laid on edge	72"	60"	48"
Nominal 2 x 6s laid on edge	108"	96"	84"

Table 4: Maximum Joist Spans for Different Sizes and Spacings

As you will see when you start to use these tables, there are many combinations that can be used in spans and spacings of joists and beams. Comparing prices for several alternatives is useful in deciding on the best one for your situation.

Table 4
MAXIMUM JOIST SPANS

	Maximum Span Per Species Group		
	A	B	C
12" Joist Spacings:			
2 x 6	10'6"	10'0"	9'0"
2 x 8	14'0"	12'6"	11'0"
2 x 10	17'6"	15'8"	13'10"
2 x 12	21'0"	19'4"	17'6"
16" Joist Spacings:			
2 x 6	9'7"	8'6"	7'7"
2 x 8	12'6"	11'0"	10'0"
2 x 10	16'2"	14'4"	13'0"
2 x 12	19'0"	18'6"	16'0"
24" Joist Spacings:			
2 x 6	8'6"	7'4"	6'8"
2 x 8	11'2"	9'9"	8'7"
2 x 10	14'0"	12'6"	11'0"
2 x 12	16'6"	16'0"	13'6"
32" Joist Spacings:			
2 x 6	7'6"	6'9"	6'0"
2 x 8	10'0"	9'1"	8'2"
2 x 10	12'10"	11'8"	10'8"
2 x 12	14'6"	14'0"	12'6"

Table 5: Maximum Spans and Spacings for Various Beam Sizes

Beams support the overall load of a deck. Remember that more beams mean more posts and foundations. This has a tendency to raise the overall cost of the deck's construction. You will find that, almost without exception, using a slightly larger beam, and thereby eliminating some of the posts and the foundations, will result in lower costs overall.

Table 5
MAXIMUM BEAM SPANS

	Maximum Span Per Species Group		
	A	B	C
48" Beam Spacing			
4 x 6	6'0"	5'10"	5'10"
3 x 8	8'0"	7'9"	7'6"
4 x 8	10'0"	9'0"	8'2"
3 x 10	11'0"	10'4"	9'6"
4 x 10	12'0"	11'4"	10'6"
3 x 12	13'0"	12'0"	11'4"
4 x 12	14'0"	13'0"	12'4"
60" Beam Spacing			
4 x 6	5'10"	5'8"	5'6"
3 x 8	7'6"	7'0"	6'8"
4 x 8	9'6"	8'6"	8'0"
3 x 10	10'6"	9'8"	9'0"
4 x 10	11'4"	10'4"	9'10"
3 x 12	12'4"	11'4"	10'6"
4 x 12	13'6"	12'6"	12'0"
72" Beam Spacing			
4 x 6	5'6"	5'5"	5'2"
3 x 8	7'0"	6'6"	6'2"
4 x 8	9'0"	8'2"	7'9"
3 x 10	10'2"	9'4"	8'9"
4 x 10	11'2"	10'2"	9'6"
3 x 12	12'0"	11'0'	10'0"
4 x 12	13'0"	12'0"	11'6"
84" Beam Spacing			
4 x 6	4'0"	4'0"	3'8"
3 x 8	6'6'	6'0"	5'10"
4 x 8	8'4"	7'10"	7'4"
3 x 10	9'8"	9'0"	8'6"
4 x 10	11'0"	10'0"	9'2"
3 x 12	11'6"	10'6"	10'6"
4 x 12	12'6"	11'6"	11'0"

Table 5, cont.
MAXIMUM BEAM SPANS

96" Beam Spacing			
3 x 8	6'2"	5'10"	5'6"
4 x 8	8'0"	7'6"	7'0"
3 x 10	9'0"	8'4"	8'0"
4 x 10	10'0"	9'4"	8'6"
3 x 12	11'0"	10'8"	10'0"
4 x 12	11'6"	10'6"	10'0"
6 x 10	12'0"	11'0"	10'6"
108" Beam Spacing			
4 x 8	7'0"	6'6"	6'0"
3 x 10	8'0"	7'4"	6'10"
4 x 10	9'0"	8'4"	7'8"
3 x 12	10'0"	9'0"	8'6"
4 x 12	10'8"	10'2"	9'6"
6 x 10	11'6"	11'0"	10'4"
120" Beam Spacing			
4 x 8	6'0"	5'8"	5'2"
3 x 10	7'0"	6'6"	6'0"
4 x 10	8'0"	7'4"	6'8"
3 x 12	9'0"	8'0"	7'6"
4 x 12	10'0"	9'6"	9'0"
6 x 10	10'6"	10'0"	9'6"
144" Beam Spacing			
3 x 10	5'2"	4'6"	4'0"
4 x 10	7'0"	6'4"	5'8"
3 x 12	8'0"	7'0"	6'4"
4 x 12	9'0"	8'4"	7'10"
6 x 10	9'6"	8'8"	8'0"

Table 6: Minimum Post Sizes for Various Sizes and Heights

The correct post size needed for your deck will depend upon the overall load area and the height of the deck that the posts will be supporting. To calculate the load area, multiply the beam spacing by the beam span. Use Table 6 on the following page to select a post size that meets the height requirements of your deck. If you have a choice, choose a post with the same thickness as the beam. This will make construction a little simpler and will give the deck a more uniform look.

Table 6
MINIMUM POST SIZES

	Maximum Load Area per Species Group		
	A	B	C
6-Foot Heights:			
4 x 4	144	144	144
4 x 6	144	144	144
6 x 6	144	144	144
8-Foot Heights:			
4 x 4	144	132	96
4 x 6	144	144	144
6 x 6	144	144	144
10-Foot Heights:			
4 x 4	108	84	60
4 x 6	144	132	96
6 x 6	144	144	144
12-Foot Heights:			
4 x 4	36	-	-
4 x 6	120	84	60
6 x 6	144	132	132

DRAWINGS

There are several drawings that may be necessary to illustrate the details of your deck. The most important of these is the *plan view*. This is the proper term for the bird's eye sketch that was discussed in Chapter 1. If your sketch is neatly done and comprehensible, and clearly shows the location of the deck on your property with all pertinent measurements, you need not draw a new one to scale. In this case, your first drawing will be a plan view of the deck only.

Plan View

Start by placing the paper on the drawing board. You will need to fasten it to the board at each corner. Drafting tape, which is similar to masking tape but isn't as sticky, is the best tape to use. Even though it will hold your paper firmly, it can easily be removed without tearing the corners of your sheet. Before you tape the paper to the board, make sure that the edges of the paper are parallel to the T-square.

To do this, slide the T-square to the top of the paper and align the top edge of the paper with the T-square (see Figure 11). Then slide the T-square down a few inches, being careful not to change the position of the paper. Tape the top two corners. Repeat this procedure for the bottom two corners. You are now ready to begin drawing.

You must decide which scale to use before you start drawing. For decks smaller than 10 feet, a scale of 1 inch representing 1 foot is ideal. For decks larger than 10 feet but smaller than 20 feet, a scale of 3/4 inch to 1 foot works well. For decks that are larger than 20 feet, a scale of 1/2 inch representing 1 foot is the best to use.

When completed, the plan view should indicate the shape and size of your deck, the surface pattern of the decking, the width of the decking material, the locations of railings, the locations of any stairways or ramps, and the locations and sizes of any other elements that you plan to include, such as benches, overheads, or planters.

If you have not yet decided the type of pattern for the deck surface, see Figure 12 for possible decking arrangements. You do not need to limit yourself to those that are illustrated, as long as you provide support under each end of each decking piece, and don't go over the maximum spans listed in the tables.

The most economical and basic surface design is that in which 2 x 4s or 2 x 6s are laid flat and perpendicular to the joists. You can minimize waste by designing the surface according to standard lumber lengths of 8, 10, 12, 14, 16, 20, and 24 feet. However, you will pay slightly more per board foot for boards that are longer than 16 feet.

If your deck design is somewhat complex, you may need other drawings that will correctly illustrate the complete construction procedure. These additional drawings could include a plan view of the substructure framing, one or more elevations, one or more elevation cross-sections, and/or detail drawings.

Plan View of Substructure Framing

See Figure 13 for an example of a plan view of substructure framing. If your deck is large or multi-level, or incorporates an unusual decking pattern, it is probably necessary to draw a plan view of the substructure framing. You should list all pertinent dimensions, including the sizes of all lumber to be used, joist and beam spacings, and methods of fastening the members together.

Elevation Drawing

An elevation drawing shows what the deck looks like as if you were standing on the side of it and looking straight at it (see Figure 14). Elevation drawings are most useful for illustrating railing designs, stairways, and height differences between levels of multi-level decks. On very complex deck designs, several elevation drawings may be necessary, each showing the deck from a different side.

Elevation Cross-Section

Elevation cross-sections are the same as elevation drawings but with one difference: a cross-section illustrates the deck as if a portion of the structure has been cut away (see Figure 15). They are commonly used to make confusing aspects of the deck clear. Cross-section drawings are quite common, and every builder is familiar with them. Some deck designs include elements that cannot be illustrated in any other way than a cross-section.

Detail Drawings

Detail drawings are frequently used to illustrate intricate details of design that are not illustrated on any other drawing (see Figure 16). Items such as exact placement of boards on benches or planters are normally shown on a special detail drawing. Any detail that is too minute to be illustrated on the other drawings should be illustrated on a separate detail drawing.

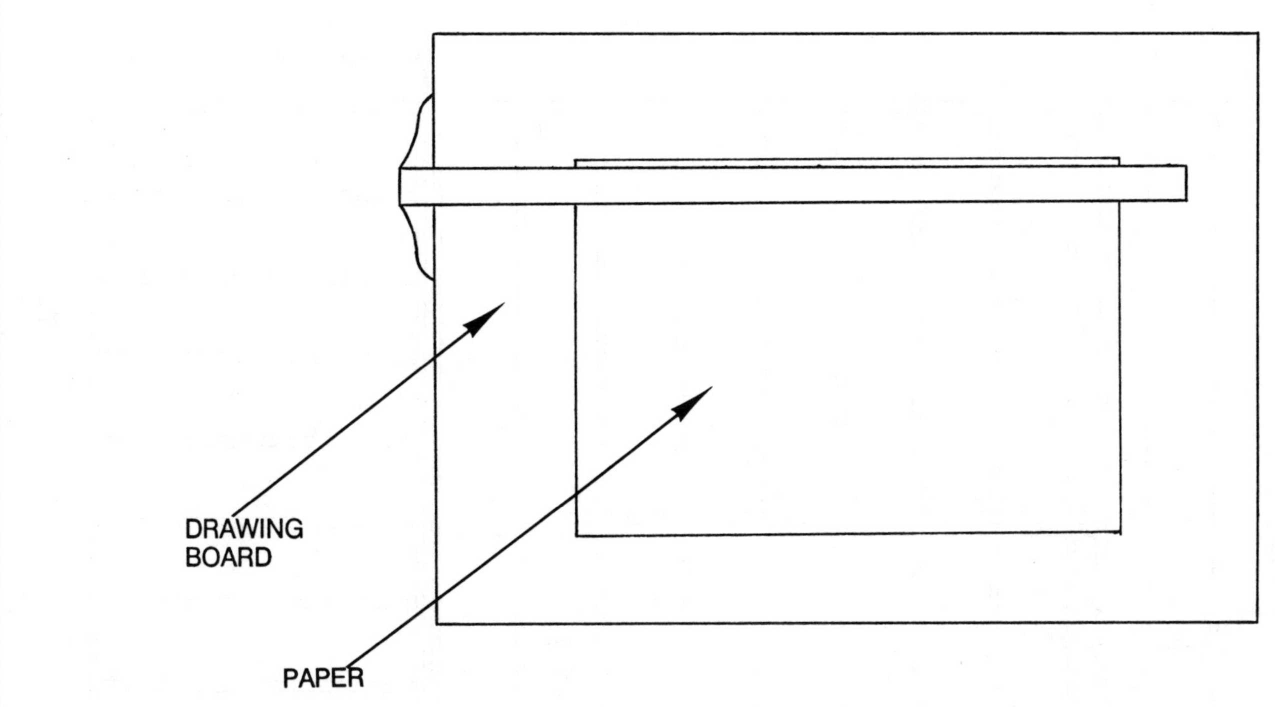

Figure 11. Before attaching the paper to the drawing board, align it parallel with the T-square.

Figure 12. Decking can be laid in any pattern you desire, provided that each decking board is supported at each end.

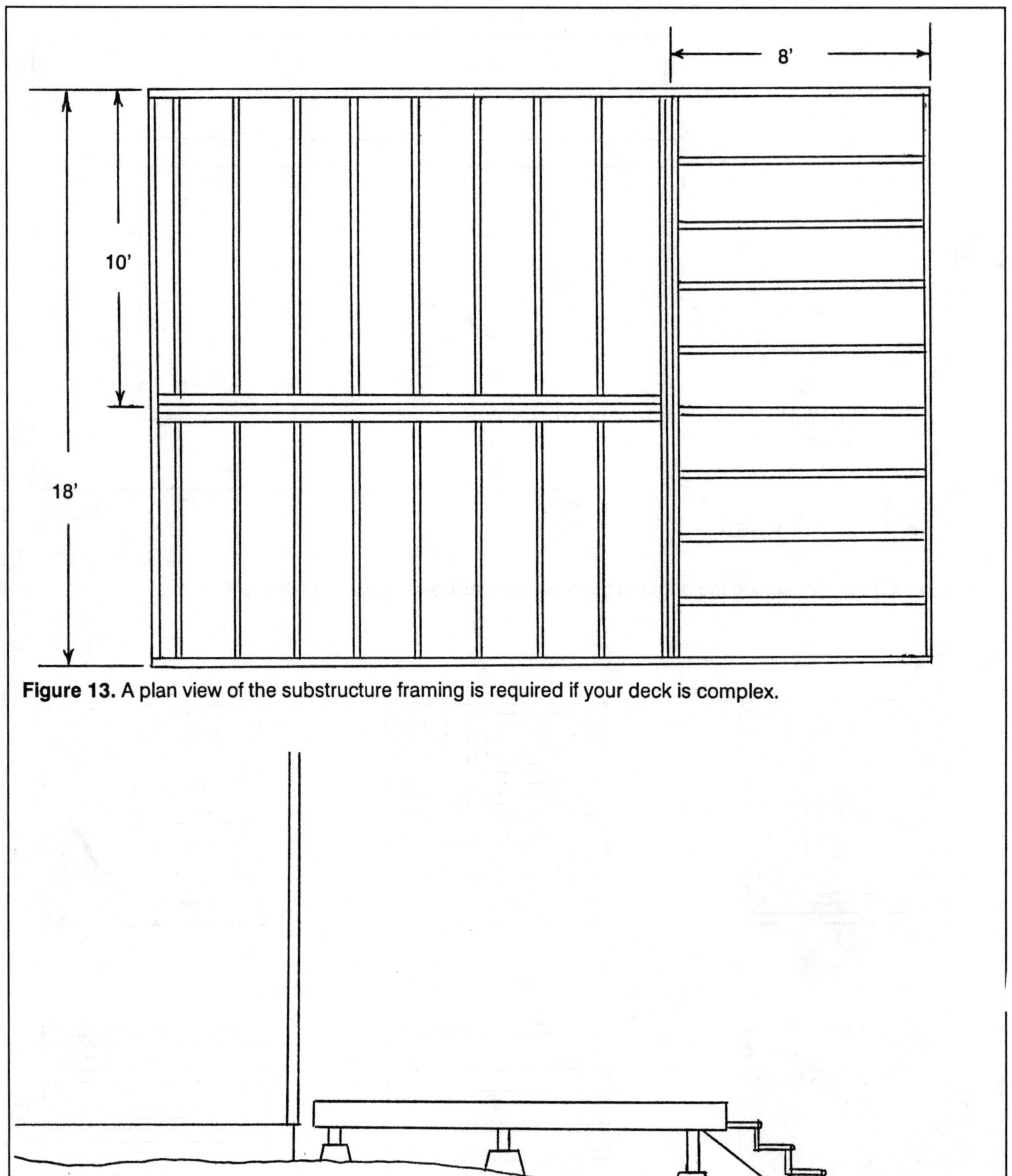

Figure 13. A plan view of the substructure framing is required if your deck is complex.

Figure 14. An elevation drawing shows what the deck will look like when you look at it directly from one side.

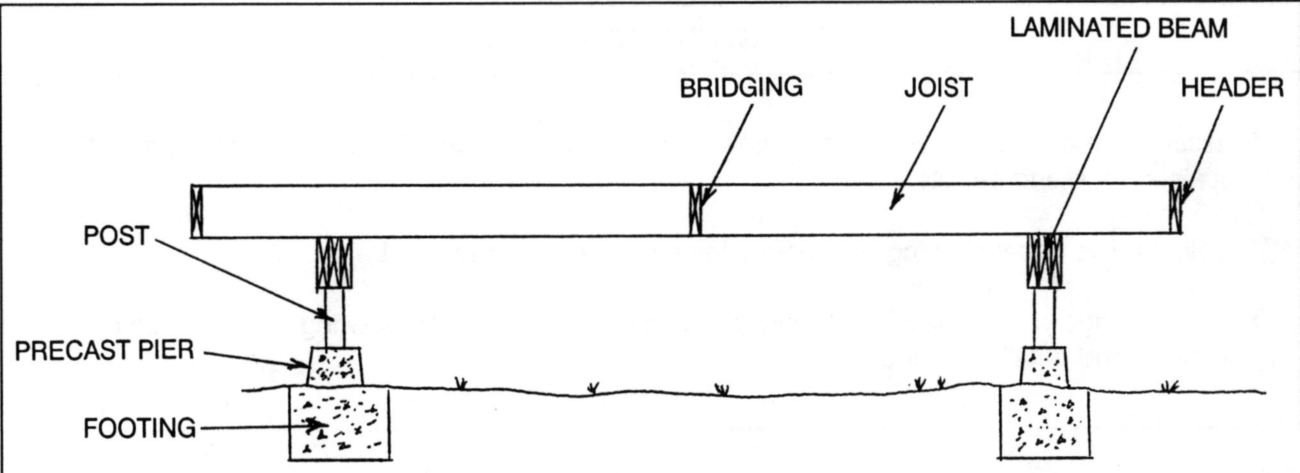

Figure 15. An elevation cross-section illustrates what the deck would look like if a portion were cut away.

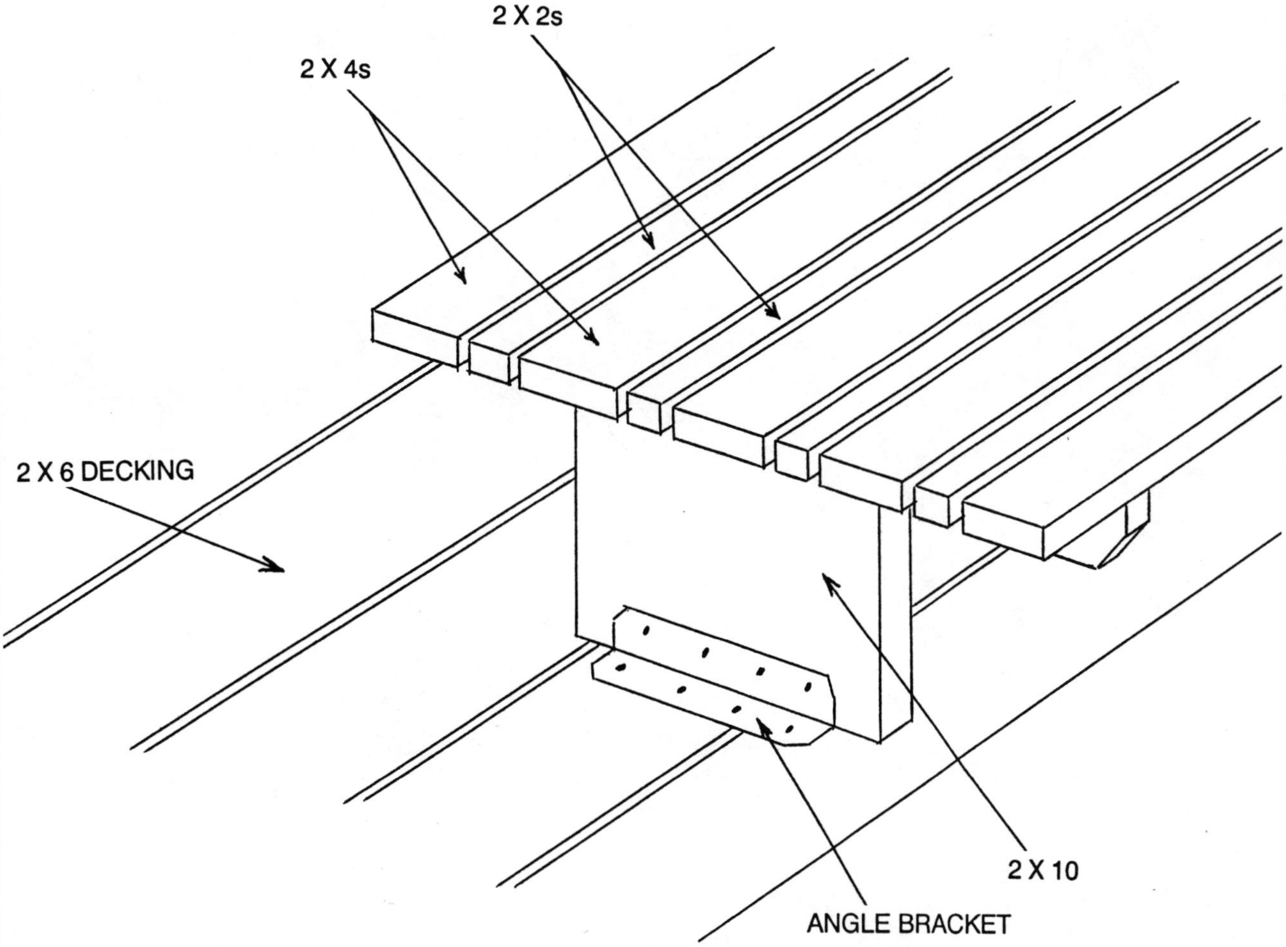

2 X 2s
2 X 4s
2 X 6 DECKING
2 X 10
ANGLE BRACKET

Figure 16. A detail drawing is used to illustrate an intricate part of the deck.

POINTS TO REMEMBER

- ❑ Assemble the tools you will need to draw a plan: drawing board, T-square, triangles, architect's scale, paper, and pencils.
- ❑ Gain a basic understanding of construction techniques before you begin.
- ❑ The drawings you will need may include a plan view, an elevation drawing, an elevation cross-section, and detail drawings.

3
Evaluating Materials

A major consideration in planning your deck is the choice of materials. Although this chapter covers briefly such materials as concrete, tile, steel, fiberglass, and outdoor carpeting, it primarily deals with wood.

It has been estimated that as many as 90% of all decks are built with wood. There are many reasons for this. Wood is lightweight, making it easy to handle. Wood resists rust, acids, saltwater, and other corrosive agents better than many other structural materials.

Wood is also very strong. Pound for pound, many species of wood are actually stronger than steel. Wood is also easy to work with. It can be cut, nailed, glued, bolted, altered, and repaired. Wood is an ideal decorative material because of its natural warmth and beauty.

Wood lends itself well to preservative treatments, and it combines easily with other materials. Finally, the last major reason that wood is so commonly used as a building material is that it is affordable.

Your choice of materials must fit well into your overall deck plan. As you contemplate different material options, be sure that their appearance will complement your home's style. If you plan to build the deck yourself, you must choose materials that you are qualified to work with. Weigh each possibility for cost, appearance, durability, and suitability to your particular situation.

ALTERNATE MATERIALS

Concrete

The majority of decks built today use concrete as the foundation material. It is strong, fireproof, relatively low in cost, and virtually maintenance-free. The drawbacks of using concrete are that it is very heavy and working with it requires hard physical labor.

It is possible to use concrete for your deck's surface. However, because concrete is so heavy, the substructure will have to be designed by an engineer. For every inch of thickness, a square foot of concrete weighs approximately 10 pounds. If a surface of the deck were made of concrete, it could easily exceed the maximum weight that the structure is designed to carry. If you choose concrete for your deck's surface, do not attempt to trowel it yourself. Concrete finishing is a specialized trade that requires much practice to develop expertise.

Tile

Surfacing a deck with tile or brick-like paving stones is among the most expensive of options. It will, however, provide a very elegant appearance. Tile is usually installed in a bed of mortar; thus a deck surface of tile is comparable in weight to one of concrete. If you choose tile for the surface of your deck, get professional design assistance.

It is possible in some instances for the homeowner to do a tile installation himself. However, to get a professional result, meticulous care is required for each tile that is installed. Do not attempt to do this type of job yourself unless you are an experienced handyman.

Steel

In certain instances, steel is an ideal material to use. It is commonly used to carry very heavy loads or to cross large spans. It will not burn, rot, or be affected by termites. It is susceptible to rust, however, and must be painted every few years.

When steel members are used as part of a deck's structure, special tools are often needed. Installation often requires welding. Steel beams that span larger distances are quite heavy, necessitating the use of a crane for their installation. If you are considering the use of steel in your deck, consult an engineer as to its design and construction.

Fiberglass

One method of obtaining a waterproof deck surface is covering it with fiberglass. With special attention given to the manufacturer's instructions, you should be able to install the fiberglass yourself. The process involves laying a specially woven fiberglass mat on your deck's clean, dry wood surface. A resin is then applied to the mat with a paint brush, covering it entirely.

One coat of resin is not sufficient—it takes several coats to make it waterproof. Each coat requires a different paint brush, as once a brush is used to apply resin it must be thrown away. Because fiberglass is so smooth, it becomes extremely slippery when wet. For this reason, in many instances the last coat of resin is covered with a light dusting of fine sand before it hardens. This gives the surface a gritty texture that greatly improves traction and reduces the likelihood of accidents.

Outdoor Carpeting

Outdoor carpeting can be an ideal surface for young children to play on. It offers good traction, is resistant to soiling, staining, and fading, and comfortably cushions any hard surface. Because it is made from synthetic materials, it is also resistant to rot, mildew, fire, and insects.

A major disadvantage of outdoor carpeting is that it requires more upkeep than other deck materials. Because it is not watertight, water can pass through it and soak the surface underneath. Water can also become trapped there. Consider this if you are planning to install outdoor carpet over a plywood base. In this instance it is advisable to use a special type of plywood, such as marine-grade (used for building boats), which is designed to withstand continuous contact with water. However, marine-grade plywood is very expensive. It may be more-cost efficient to use regular plywood and cover it with fiberglass. Compare the alternatives.

DECK HARDWARE

Lumberyards and building supply stores carry a wide range of fasteners and connectors specially designed both to simplify and to strengthen deck construction. This section will help you become familiar with the many products available.

Nails

There are many varieties of nails. Four that are frequently used in deck construction are: common, box, finish, and ring (see Figure 18). For exterior use do not use an uncoated steel nail. The trade name for these is "bright." They will quickly rust and stain your deck. After a short period of time, the rust will weaken the nail to such a degree that it no longer has any holding power.

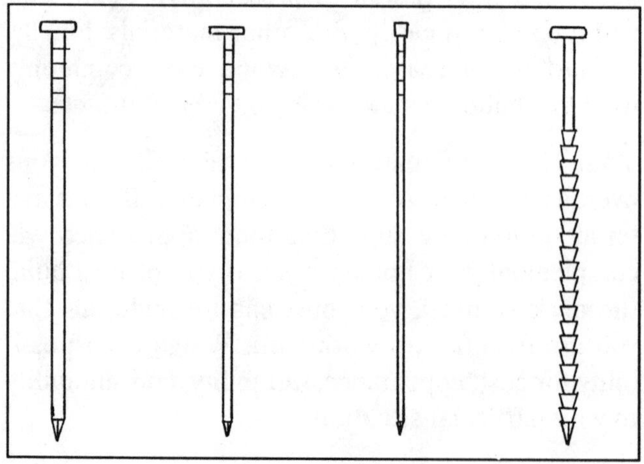

Figure 18. The four types of nails shown are from left to right: common, box, finish, and ring.

A better choice is a nail that has a galvanized coating. This protects the steel from moisture and is supposed to prevent the nail from rusting. However, when you pound these nails in, often the force of the hammer will cause the galvanized coating to fall off the head of the nail. The exposed head quickly rusts.

Some companies try to prevent this from occurring by double dipping the nails in molten zinc. This coats the nails twice, giving them double protection from moisture. I have found that even these nails will rust a couple of years after their installation.

The most effective way to prevent nails from rusting is to purchase stainless steel or aluminum nails. Although both cost considerably more than galvanized nails, aluminum nails are less expensive than their steel counterparts. However, aluminum is not as strong as steel, and in some species of wood the aluminum nails won't go through the board; they simply bend. In these instances it may be necessary to drill pilot holes before pounding in the nails. This is not usually required for stainless steel nails.

Nails come in many sizes, and sizes are indicated in terms of "penny." The abbreviation for penny is "d", from the ancient Roman coin that was equivalent to a penny, the *denarius*. The chart below lists lengths for different size nails, and the approximate number of nails per pound.

NAIL SIZES AND COUNTS

Penny Size	Length in Inches	Number of Nails per Pound Common	Box	Finish
2d	1	875	1,000	1,350
3d	1 1/4	565	635	800
4d	1 1/2	315	475	585
6d	2	180	235	310
8d	2 1/2	105	145	190
10d	3	70	95	120
12d	3 1/4	62	90	115
16d	3 1/2	50	70	90
20d	4	30	51	63
30d	4 1/2	23	45	—
40d	5	17	35	—
50d	5 1/2	13	—	—
60d	6	11	—	—

Common nails are used in nearly every aspect of deck construction because of their thick shanks and large heads. Box nails are similar in design to common nails, but their shanks are smaller in diameter. Finish nails are used in applications that are primarily cosmetic. Because of their small heads and extra-narrow shanks, they lack structural holding power. Nails with maximum holding power are those with ring shanks. Because they hold so well, it is difficult to pull them out. (To do so, see the section in Chapter 5 that deals with this topic.)

If your deck plans call for extensive nailing, you might want to consider renting a pneumatic nailer. These run on compressed air and are capable of driving from three to eight nails per second. The amount of time saved using one of these tools is considerable. However, they do need nails that are joined together in stick or coil form, and most will only accept nails that are manufactured by the company that made the tool. These nails cost more than standard nails.

Screws

Nearly all screws have superior holding power over any type of nail. If your decking needs to be fastened very securely, it's best to use a galvanized deck screw. These require a Phillips screwdriver for their installation. It is nearly impossible to put these screws in by hand. A much more efficient method is to buy a Phillips screw tip for use in an electric drill. Installation of this in your drill will give you a very speedy method for fastening your deck with screws. Some species of wood split when you use screws in them; it may be necessary to pre-drill pilot holes to keep this from happening.

Bolts

Where maximum strength is of primary importance, bolts are the ideal fastener to use. They come in a myriad of lengths and diameters. For outdoor applications, it is unwise to use any bolt that has not been galvanized. Stainless steel bolts are preferable, although they are more expensive and will probably have to be special ordered.

You will need to purchase bolts that are at least 1

inch longer than the thickness of the two pieces to be joined together. This gives you enough room to include a flat washer on each side and allows the nut to be completely on the threaded part of the bolt, ensuring strong holding power.

Lag screws are similar to bolts, except that they screw into the wood and do not use nuts. They are ideal for use when you are working in cramped locations and can only reach one side of the piece. Socket sets are the most efficient tools for installing bolts and lag screws, although the installation can be done with ordinary wrenches.

Joist Hangers

Joist hangers are commonly used to connect a joist to a header or beam (see Figure 19). They are available at nearly all building supply outlets and come in many sizes to fit most standard lumber dimensions. When using joist hangers, make sure that the manufacturer's instructions for installation are followed exactly. The joist hanger should be securely fastened to both of the pieces that it connects.

Post and Beam Connectors

These metal connectors sit on top of a post. They are attached securely to the post and to the beam that rests on the post (see Figure 20). By using this type of connector, you will be able to simplify the construction process, as well as strengthen the deck.

Post Anchors

These are installed in the concrete foundation before the concrete has hardened (see Figure 21). They come in several sizes to accommodate different sizes of posts. They are an excellent method for securely fastening posts to the foundation. They are used most often in wet areas where the post should be kept above ground level to protect it from rapid deterioration.

WOOD BASICS

Acquiring a fundamental knowledge of lumber, and how it gets from stump to store, will help you in your decision to choose materials suited to your needs. It will also help you communicate your needs to the personnel at lumberyards.

All lumber comes from wood that falls into two categories: hardwood, which comes from deciduous trees (those that shed their leaves annually); and softwood, which comes from conifers (evergreen trees that keep their needles year-round). The terms hardwood and softwood do not actually indicate the hardness or softness of the wood. A few species of hardwood are actually softer than some species of softwood. In general, though, hardwood is harder than softwood.

Each species, whether hardwood or softwood, contains heartwood and sapwood (see Figure 22). Heartwood is the dense inner part of the tree that is not living. Because it is dense and not living, the heartwood is more stable, stronger, and harder, providing strength and rigidity to the tree.

Sapwood is the living outer part of a tree. It carries water from the soil, which enters the tree through its roots, up to the leaves. Because sapwood has a higher water content, it will shrink more when dried and has a greater tendency to develop defects during the drying process.

Just outside the sapwood, and just inside the bark, is the cambium. This layer produces a new ring of wood every year. The life story of the tree can be read in its rings. When growing conditions are favorable, the new ring will be wide. When there is a shortage of food and water, the rings are narrow.

Some commonly used species of hardwood are oak, maple, walnut, mahogany, birch, and cherry. Hardwood is usually more expensive than softwood, and it is more difficult to work with. Compared to cutting softwood, saw blades become dull much sooner when they are used to cut hardwood. It is also very difficult to pound nails through most types of hardwood. For these reasons, hardwood is rarely used in deck construction, but commonly used to make furniture and cabinets.

There are many species of softwoods that are commercially harvested for use as lumber. The table below lists some of the more widely used species of softwood. A commercial name for lumber sometimes includes more than one species.

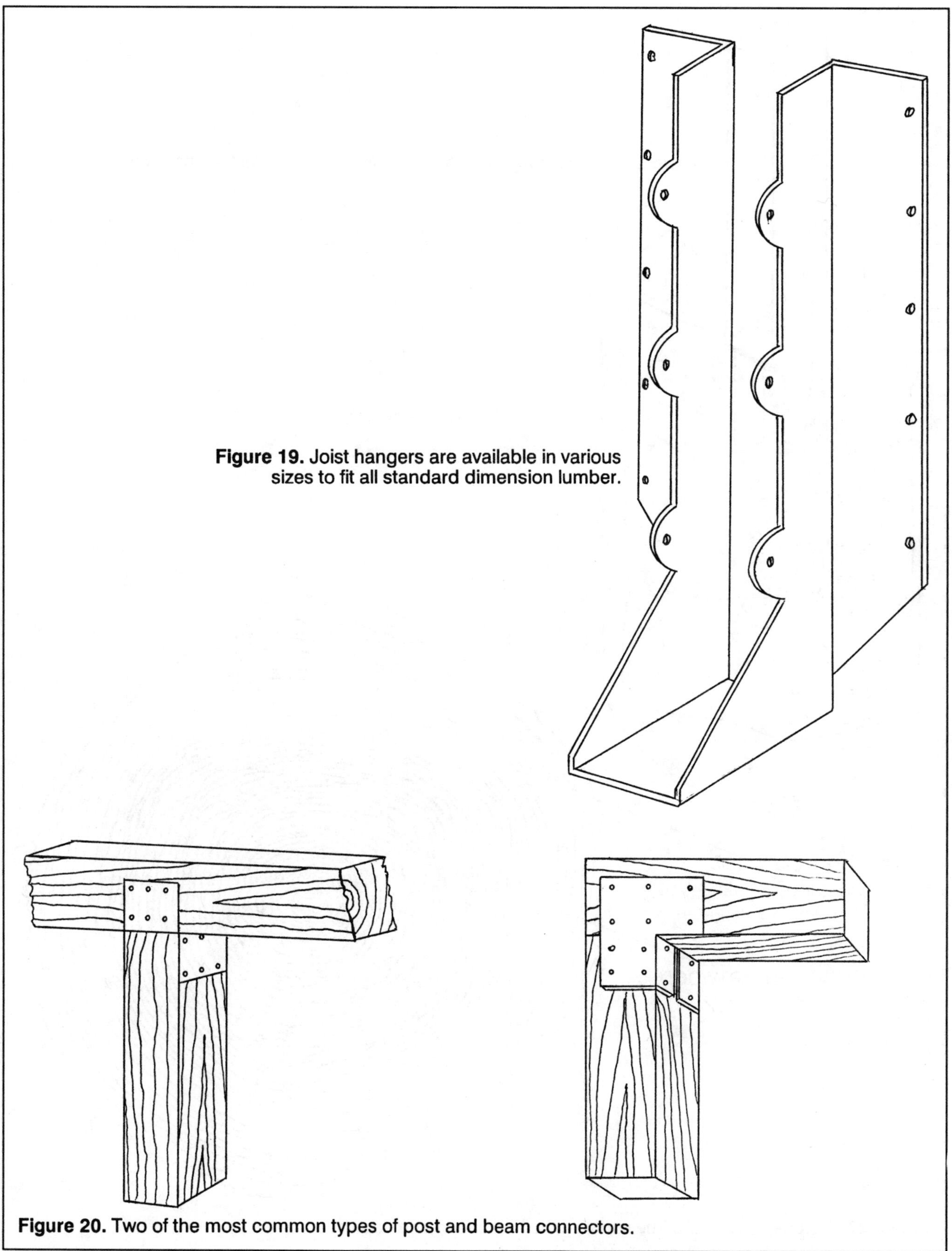

Figure 19. Joist hangers are available in various sizes to fit all standard dimension lumber.

Figure 20. Two of the most common types of post and beam connectors.

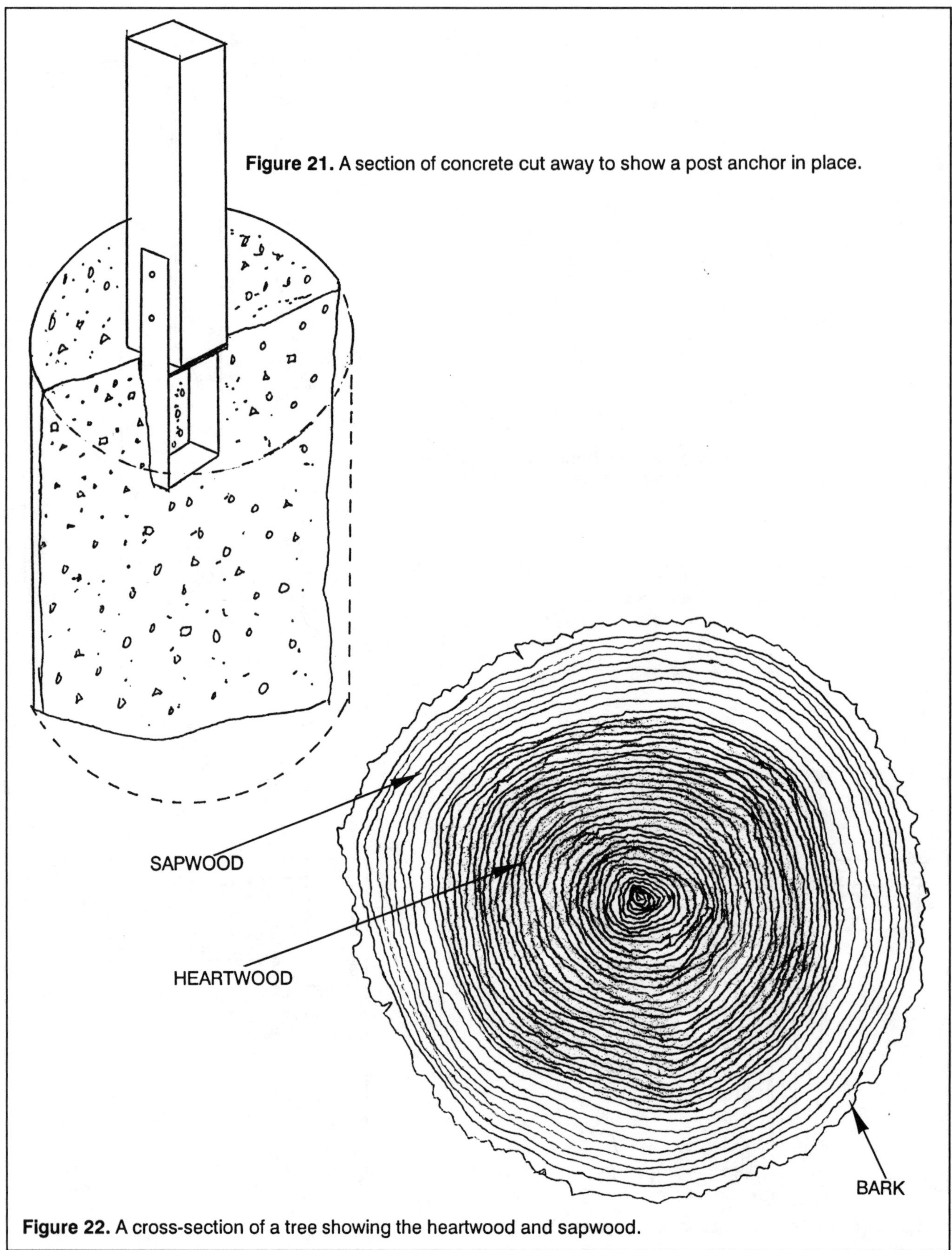

Figure 21. A section of concrete cut away to show a post anchor in place.

Figure 22. A cross-section of a tree showing the heartwood and sapwood.

NAMES FOR DIFFERENT WOOD SPECIES

Commercial Lumber Name	Common Tree	Botanical Name
Alaska Cedar	Alaska cedar	*Chamaecyparis Nootkatensis*
Auromic Red Cedar	Incense cedar	*Libocedrus Decurrens*
Eastern Red Cedar	Eastern red cedar	*Juniperus Virginiana*
	Southern red cedar	*Juniperus Silicicola*
Western Red Cedar	Western red cedar	*Thuja Plicata*
Northern White Cedar	Northern white cedar	*Thuja Occidentalis*
Southern White Cedar	Atlantic white cedar	*Chamaecyparis Thyoides*
Cypress	Bald cypress	*Taxodium Distichum*
	Pond cypress	*Taxodium Distichum Nutans Var.*
Balsam Fir	Balsam fir	*Abies Balsamea*
	Fraser fir	*Abies Fraseri*
Douglas Fir	Douglas fir	*Pseudotsuga Menziesii*
White Fir	California red fir	*Abies Magnifica*
	Grand fir	*Abies Grandis*
	Noble fir	*Abies Procera*
	White fir	*Abies Concolor*
Eastern Hemlock	Carolina hemlock	*Tsuga Caroliniana*
	Eastern hemlock	*Tsuga Canadensis*
West Coast Hemlock	Western hemlock	*Tsuga Heterophylla*
Western Juniper	Alligator juniper	*Juniperus Deppeana*
	Rocky Mountain juniper	*Juniperus Scopulorum*
	Western juniper	*Juniperus Occidentalis*
Western Larch	Western larch	*Larix Occidentalis*
Lodgepole Pine	Lodgepole pine	*Pinus Contorta*
Norway Pine	Red pine	*Pinus Resinosa*
Ponderosa Pine	Ponderosa pine	*Pinus Ponderosa*
Sugar Pine	Sugar pine	*Pinus Lambertiana*
Northern White Pine	Eastern white pine	*Pinus Strobus*
Southern Yellow Pine	Longleaf pine	*Pinus Palustris*
	Loblolly pine	*Pinus Taeda*
	Pitch pine	*Pinus Rigida*
	Slash pine	*Pinus Eliottii*
	Virginia pine	*Pinus Virginiana*
Redwood	Redwood	*Sequoia Sempervirens*
Eastern Spruce	Black spruce	*Picea Mariana*
	Red spruce	*Picea Rubens*
	White spruce	*Picea Glauca*
Sitka Spruce	Sitka spruce	*Picea Sitchensis*

Moisture Content

Moisture content, expressed as a percentage, is the measurement of the amount of water that is contained in wood. The lower the percentage, the drier the wood. As wood dries, it loses water contained in the cell cavities first. When the moisture content gets down around 27%, the cell walls begin to lose water.

At this point wood begins to shrink in width and length. The majority of the shrinkage is in the width. The shrinkage in length is so small that it is not considered a problem, but the shrinkage in width is considerable and can cause many problems.

It is important to buy wood that has been dried. As wood dries, it develops defects, such as warping, as a result of the water leaving the cell walls. The majority of these defects will develop only during the original drying process. After it has been dried, wood will continue to pick up or give off moisture until it balances with the humidity in the surrounding air. However, as it goes through these seasonal changes, such as from a damp season to a dry season, it usually does not develop any new defects.

Seasoning

When wood is freshly cut, it contains as much as 300% more water than it has after it dries. Wood that has not dried is said to be "green." There are two methods for drying lumber: air drying and kiln drying. Air drying is done outside. Wood is stacked in layers. In between each layer are crosspieces called "stickers." These are used to create an air space between each layer. This is necessary to get adequate ventilation around each board, allowing the boards to dry in a shorter period of time.

When lumber is kiln dried, it is stacked in the same manner as when air dried. It is then placed in a giant oven, called a "kiln." The humidity and temperature are both carefully controlled. When the wood is first placed in the kiln, there is low heat and high humidity. Gradually the heat is turned up, and the humidity reduced, until there is high heat and low humidity in the kiln. The process takes only three to five days, compared to up to one year for air drying. However, it does add to the cost of the lumber, as the kiln-drying process is expensive.

Lumber Grading

Lumber is classified in grades, and the grading is done by specialists. They consider about twenty-five different factors, conditions, and defects of the wood. This enables the purchaser to know the quality of the wood that he buys. In general, a board with fewer defects in it receives a higher grade and is more expensive.

Stress-Grade Lumber

Each species of wood has been stress-graded. The results of stress-grading tests are used to compile tables such as the one in Chapter 2. To obtain a stress-grade, lumber is precisely tested as it is subjected to a variety of external forces or loads. These loads are considered "live" or "dead."

Dead load is the weight of the materials in the structure itself, and its share of the total weight of the remainder of the structure. For example, the dead load of a deck would be the weight of the joists, the decking, and any built-in benches or railings.

Live load refers to the forces or weight applied to the deck. These may be static, impact, or repetitive. Static loads are those that remain constant. An example is deck furniture. Repetitive loads are those to which a surface is subjected a number of times. An example of repetitive loads is people walking across the deck.

Impact loads are the result of a sudden stress placed on the deck, such as that from a tree falling. To handle live and dead loads, wood must have certain strength properties. Stress-graded lumber has been tested for its ability to withstand stresses caused by loads. The most common stresses are compressive, shear, and tensile (see Figure 23).

Most lumberyards do not carry boards that have been individually stress-graded, although they usually can special order them upon request. Boards will be of proper strength if the tables in Chapter 2 are used to determine their sizes.

Common Defects

You should try to avoid some of the more common and obvious defects that occur in lumber. Most

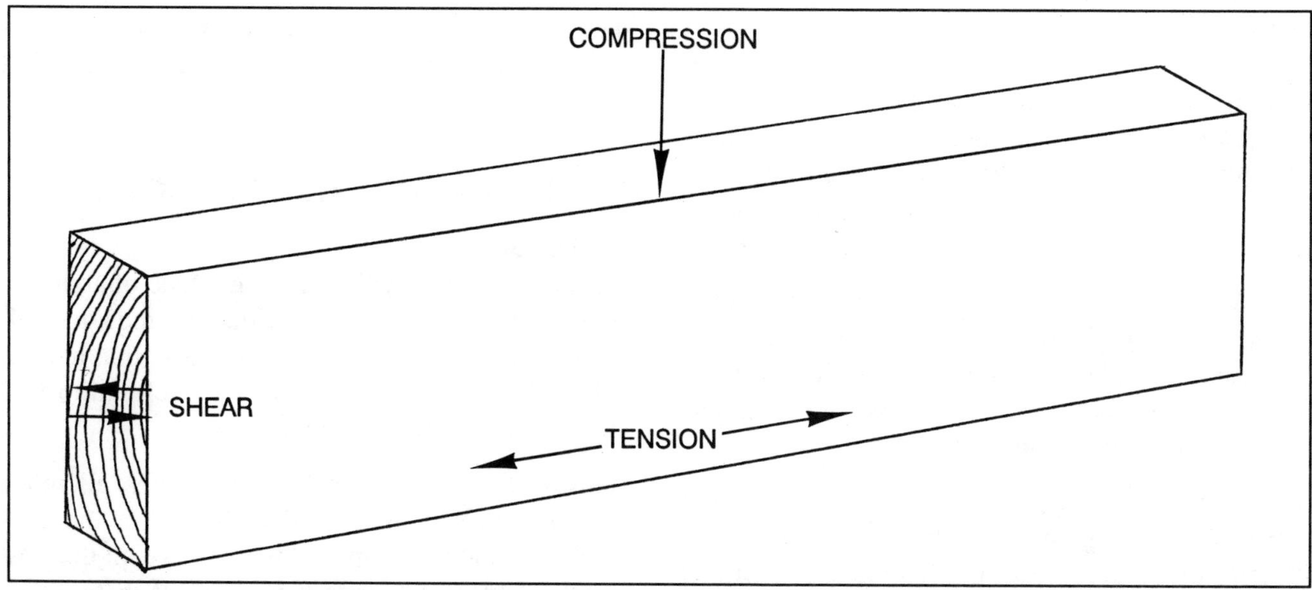

Figure 23. The various stresses on a joist or beam.

lumberyards will allow you to hand-pick each piece that you are purchasing. If you call in your order and the lumberyard delivers it, you will probably be allowed to return any piece that is not satisfactory. Some of the defects to look for are:

CHECK. This is lengthwise grain separation or splitting. It usually occurs at the end of a piece as a result of the drying process.

DECAY. This is the disintegration of the wood caused by fungi or bacteria that destroy the wood.

LOOSE OR MISSING KNOTS. Branches become embedded in, and part of, the tree as it grows. As boards are sawn from the logs, these branches are cut through and form knots. When wood dries, the knots can become loose and even fall out.

PITCH POCKET. This is an opening in the wood, usually between the growth rings, that contains a large amount of resin, or pitch.

SPLIT. This is a separation in the wood grain that runs lengthwise. If the separation does not penetrate the entire thickness of the board, it is called a *shake*.

STAIN. This is discoloration in the lumber. It usually occurs when logs are left for a long period of time before being sawn into boards.

TORN GRAIN. Before logs are sawn into boards, the bark is removed. Large, powerful machines roll the log around, scraping off the bark. During this process the log can get jammed in the machine, causing the grain to be torn.

WANE. Because trees are round, boards that are cut from the outside of the log sometimes have an edge that is rounded. The rounded edge may or may not contain bark. This imperfection is called a wane.

WARP. This is a variation from a straight edge or surface. The three different types of warps are: bow, crook, and cup (see Figure 24).

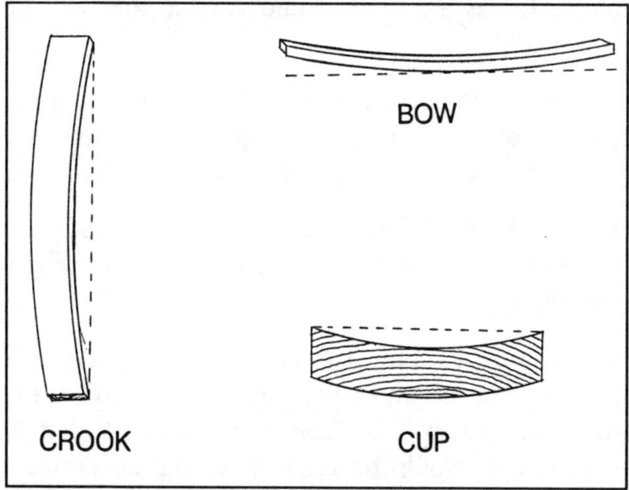

Figure 24. Three ways that a board can warp.

Plywood

Plywood is made by gluing wood layers together. The grain of each layer is usually perpendicular to the grain of the nearest layer on each side. These thin wood layers are made by slicing the wood from a log. The process involves a huge lathe and giant tongs.

The log is clamped into place on the lathe and is spun swiftly. As the log revolves, a long, razor-like blade cuts into the log and peels off a thin continuous strip of wood. This process looks similar to paper being unwound from a roll.

Depending on the type of glue used to bond these layers of wood together, the plywood is classified as interior or exterior. Exterior plywood is guaranteed not to become unglued and delaminate. It is the only acceptable grade for exterior use.

Each face, or side, of plywood is graded according to the number of defects that it contains. The grades range from N, the highest grade, to D, the lowest grade. The definition of each grade is as follows:

N. This grade is intended for natural finish. It is free of open defects and permits only very minor repairs. Veneers in this grade are made from either all heartwood or all sapwood.

A. This grade is smooth, knot-free, and paintable. Neatly made repairs are permissible and common. This can also be used for a natural finish where the top quality is not necessary.

B. This grade allows some tight knots and repair plugs. It has a smooth, solid surface and can be painted.

C. This grade permits some defects that do not impair the overall strength of the panel. Knotholes are allowed to be missing up to 1 1/2 inches in diameter.

D. This is the lowest grade. It permits knots and holes up to 2 1/2 inches. Splits in the veneer are also permitted.

If you are planning a fiberglass deck, you would probably choose plywood graded A-C or B-C. If the deck surface will be concrete, plywood that is graded C-D would be used under the concrete. If you order plywood and need to store it for a few days before you use it, be sure to store it flat. If it is stored on an angle, such as leaning against a wall, it will warp.

COMMON WOOD CHOICES FOR DECKS

Redwood

Redwood fits well with almost any style of architecture. The reddish hue is unique to redwood, although over a period of time it will lose that natural color and turn to a silvery gray if it is left unfinished and exposed to the elements.

Redwood is the standard against which all other deck materials are measured. It can also be the most expensive material, especially if you live on the East Coast. However, it does pay for itself in terms of longevity and attractiveness. You can use redwood for all parts of the deck, but to save money you may choose to use it only for the parts that will show.

Clear Heartwood is the best grade, and it is highly resistant to the natural attack of the elements. Some of the lower grades contain sapwood, which isn't as resistant as heartwood. Redwood is quite soft and is easy to work with. The downside of this is that it is easily damaged. Redwood dents readily when something is dropped on it.

Pressure-Treated Wood

Several species of softwood that aren't naturally resistant to the elements are available with factory impregnated preservatives. Chemical preservatives are used to give woods such as Fir or Southern Yellow Pine the ability to withstand the elements for decades.

Many manufacturers of pressure-treated lumber guarantee their product for up to forty years. They can do so because wood that has been treated in this manner is extremely resistant to rot and decay. The preservatives used in the process are driven into the wood with great pressure, fully penetrating each board. That is where the term "pressure-treated" originates.

The chemicals used to treat the lumber give it a greenish color, as the chemicals are driven in and absorbed by the cell walls in the lumber. This makes pressure-treated lumber denser and therefore heavier and stronger than untreated softwood. However, because it is denser it is harder, making pressure-treated lumber more difficult to work with.

Pressure-treated lumber is very hard to cut and requires a new or recently sharpened saw blade. Driving nails through pressure-treated wood is also rather difficult. It may be necessary to drill pilot holes in the lumber in order to drive a nail through a board without bending the nail or splitting the wood.

When left uncovered and exposed to the elements, pressure-treated lumber loses its greenish color and weathers to gray. With some types of treated wood, it is necessary to let it weather for one year before you stain or paint it. With these types of pressure-treated wood, the stain or paint would not bond if you tried to apply it to lumber that has not been allowed to weather.

When working with pressure-treated lumber, it is necessary to follow the safety precautions issued by the manufacturer. Many types of pressure-treated lumber use toxic materials in the treatment process. You may be required to use gloves and safety glasses when working with the lumber. Because of the toxic substances that it may contain, never attempt to burn pressure-treated lumber. The fumes could be poisonous.

Pressure-treated lumber is usually somewhat less expensive than redwood, and it is available in all areas of the country. When used, it makes a strong and durable deck, and it offers good value for the money.

Cedar and Cypress

Cedar and cypress have a more rustic look than redwood. Their color has more of a burnt-orange tint to it. Both are naturally resistant to the elements, as is redwood, but both are denser than redwood, making them stronger. However, they are not nearly as strong as pressure-treated lumber.

Working with cedar or cypress is very similar to working with redwood. These woods are quite easy to cut and nail, making them a good choice as decking material. The price is also appealing, as they are less expensive than redwood, especially in areas of the country away from the West Coast.

Untreated Pine, Fir, Hemlock, and Spruce

A choice of one of these would be the least expensive route to take but might not be the best value for your dollar. None offers natural resistance to the elements. Unless special care is taken, these woods would have to be replaced in a relatively short period of time.

If you are on a tight budget, and don't mind the extra maintenance required for a deck built with one of these species of lumber, this is the most economical alternative. Any of these woods gives you the lowest cost per square foot of deck, allowing you to build a larger deck for less money. However, you will need to pay special attention to the advice in Chapter 8 on maintaining your deck.

Points to Remember

- ❑ Special alternate materials to consider include concrete, tile, steel, fiberglass, and outdoor carpeting.
- ❑ Become familiar with the types of deck hardware, including varieties of nails and screws, bolts, joist hangers, post and beam connectors, and post anchors.
- ❑ Gain a working understanding of wood basics, including moisture content, seasoning, lumber grading, and common defects.
- ❑ Among common wood choices for decks are redwood, pressure-treated lumber, cedar, and cypress.

4
Purchasing Materials

Estimating involves figuring out the quantity of materials you will need to complete your project. Depending on your deck's design, this may be a complex task. This chapter will break down the estimating process into several components, making the procedure easier and ensuring that no item is left out.

If you casually perform the estimates in this chapter, you are apt to have more waste than necessary. Meticulously planning and figuring your material needs, while paying careful attention to using various board sizes as efficiently as possible, will save you money.

It is necessary to refer constantly to your working scale drawings as you calculate the quantity of materials that you need. If you hired a drafter or designer to draw your plans, you will find many abbreviations on the plans. Lumberyards also use abbreviations extensively.

As you make your detailed material list, you may find it convenient to use the typical abbreviations of the trade. The table on the next page contains some of the more common abbreviations likely to appear on your plans or in price quotes that you receive from the building supply outlets. This is not a complete list, but it probably includes the majority of the abbreviations you are likely to come across.

ESTIMATING MATERIALS

Estimating materials is a matter of counting and recording the individual items necessary to complete your deck project. At the end of this chapter you will find a form to use to record the different items as you calculate the quantities of each.

Once completed, this form will be a detailed list of the materials you'll need. In the trade this list is called a *take off*. You will be able to take this list to several building outlets in your area to get exact price quotes. For this purpose, it's best to be as specific as possible when listing each individual item.

For example, instead of listing your needs for joists as: 10—2" x 10" x 8', it would be better to list them as: 10—2" x 10" x 8' KD spruce or fir, No. 2 or better. This allows the lumberyards to give you a price for the exact item you want. By doing so, you can compare prices for identical items at each lumberyard, giving you an accurate assessment of which actually offers the best prices.

Before you start the estimating process, make several copies of the worksheets and forms at the end of this chapter, get a couple of pencils, and have handy your set of scale drawings. It is best to save the worksheets that you use to do your calculating. This is especially true if your deck plan is a complex one, involving several deck surfaces or stairs.

Your worksheet will contain information valuable to you when you start building your deck. In order to get a better price, it is likely that you will be ordering a large quantity of materials at once from a supplier. By doing so, you'll be able to get a volume discount.

LUMBERYARD ABBREVIATIONS

APA — American Plywood Association
AIA — American Institute of Architects
AIBD — American Institute of Building Designers
ALS — American Lumber Standards
AVG — Average
AWPB — American Wood Preservers Bureau
AW&L — All widths and lengths
BD — Board
BD FT — Board feet
BDL — Bundle
BEV — Bevel
BOCA — Building Officials Code Administration
BTR — Better
C/L — Carload
CLG — Ceiling
CLR — Clear
CSG — Casing
d — Penny
DF — Douglas Fir
DIM — Dimension
DKG — Decking
FLG — Flooring
FRT — Freight
Ft — Foot
Gal. — Gallon
Galv. — Galvanized
GRN — Green
HEM — Hemlock
IN — Inch
IWP — Idaho White Pine
KD — Kiln dried
Lb. — Pound
LBR — Lumber
LF — Linear feet
LGR — Longer
LGTH — Length
LIN — Linear
LP — Lodgepole Pine
M — Thousand
MBF — Thousand Board Feet
MC — Moisture content
MG — Mixed grain
MISC — Miscellaneous
MLDG — Molding
MSR — Machine stress rated
NBM — Net board measure
No. — Number
NWP — Northern White Pine
PAD — Partially air dried
PARA — Paragraph
PART — Partition
PAT — Pattern
Pcs. — Pieces
PP — Ponderosa Pine
PT — Pressure treated
P&T — Posts and timbers
RC — Red Cedar
RDM — Random
REG — Regular
RGH — Rough
R.O. — Rough opening
R/L — Random lengths
R/W — Random widths
SDG — Siding
S/L — Shiplap
SM — Surface measure
SQ — Square
STK — Stock
STPG — Stepping
STR — Structural
SYP — Southern Yellow Pine
S2E — Surfaced two edges
S1S — Surfaced one side
S4S — Surfaced four sides
TBR — Timber
T&G — Tongue and groove
UBC — Uniform Building Code
WDR — Wider
WF — White Fir
WT — Weight
WTH — Width
WRC — Western Red Cedar
WWPA — Western Wood Products Association

Your worksheet will contain all the details of where each different size board will be used. This information may not necessarily be listed on the working drawings. You determine what length lumber to use as you estimate the materials for each component. For future use, be sure to record that information in understandable fashion on your worksheet.

Foundation

To estimate the amount of concrete that you will need, you must first understand some basic elements of concrete. Please go to Chapter 5 and read the section that deals with pouring concrete foundations. This will give you a basic understanding of concrete.

If your plans call for digging a hole to place the foundation in, don't forget to figure materials to build the forms. Sonotubes are ideal for this task. They are specially designed for pouring foundation columns, and are available in sizes from 8 to 24 inches in diameter.

You can figure the concrete needed in either cubic feet or cubic yards. A cubic foot is the volume in a box that is 1 foot long by 1 foot wide by 1 foot high. A cubic yard is the volume in a box that is 3 feet long by 3 feet wide by 3 feet high. There are 27 cubic feet in 1 cubic yard.

If all your foundation footings and piers will be the same size, you merely have to figure the volume of one and multiply by the number there will be. This will give you the total volume of concrete you will need. If your plans call for several different sizes, figure the volume for each one and add the volumes together to get the total amount needed.

When figuring the volume of the foundation, treat odd-shaped areas as though they were rectangular. For example, if you are trying to figure the volume of a sonotube that is 8 inches in diameter, figure it as though it were 8 inches square. In these instances only, it is not necessary to figure the precise amount of volume. By figuring shapes such as cylinders and pyramids as though they were rectangular, your estimates will be close enough.

Also, to simplify the process, avoid using cubic inches to figure volume. To do this, simply convert inches into decimal equivalents of feet. For example, if your footing measured 8 inches by 10 inches by 15 inches, the volume would be .67 times .83 times 1.25 = .70 cubic feet. When you are done figuring the volume of concrete required, add 10 to 20% to be sure that you'll have enough.

If the total of your concrete needs is a very small amount, say less than 6 or 7 cubic feet, the easiest way to purchase it is in premixed 90-pound bags. Each bag will make about 2/3 of a cubic foot. If you need slightly more concrete but less than 20 cubic feet, it is worth your time to mix the ingredients yourself. You can purchase the cement in 94-pound bags. These are the equivalent of 1 cubic foot.

The sand and crushed stone can also be purchased in bags. The most economical size is 100 pounds. You must purchase two bags of sand for every bag of cement that you buy, and three bags of crushed stone for each bag of cement. If you have access to a pickup truck, it will cost much less to drive to a local gravel pit and buy the materials there. Typically, the charge is $10 for all the sand or stone that your pickup will carry.

If your foundation requires more than 20 cubic feet of concrete, you can order the sand and crushed stone in bulk quantities from an excavation contractor. Minimum orders are usually 1 cubic yard or 1 ton, although this varies from contractor to contractor. Some may add an extra charge for small orders. Shop around for the best deal.

For large foundations, which require more than 1 cubic yard of concrete, ordering transit-mixed concrete may be the best alternative. However, you may have to pay fees in addition to the price of the concrete, which is about $60 per cubic yard. Some companies add an extra charge if you purchase less than 3 yards. This fee will probably range from $25 to $50.

If your pour is not continuous, the company may also charge a "truck fee." You are allowed approximately 20 to 30 minutes to pour the concrete. If your pour takes longer than that, expect to pay about $40 per hour for the additional time that the truck is at your job site.

It is important to consider a couple of additional factors if you are planning to order transit-mixed concrete. The trucks that deliver the concrete are extremely heavy. They weigh from 40,000 to 80,000 pounds each, depending upon how much concrete they are carrying. If they have to drive across a lawn or garden to get to the place where you want the concrete unloaded, they will sink into the ground and cause damage. This is especially true in the spring when the ground is softer because it contains more water. If a truck gets stuck in your yard, you will have to pay the towing fee to have it removed.

If you plan to have the concrete delivered in this manner, do not schedule a delivery until you are certain that you will be completely prepared for the concrete when it arrives. This includes having all the foundation holes dug, all the forms built, and a team ready to help you unload the concrete. Do not attempt to unload the concrete alone. Concrete weighs about 125 pounds per cubic foot. You will need assistance to place the concrete where it needs to be. Plan on having at least one or two people help you. The tools required are a heavy-duty wheelbarrow, one or two buckets, and a couple of shovels.

Do not expect the driver to help you unload the concrete. He is a driver, not a laborer. He does not get paid to do the physical labor involved in unloading the truck. He will merely operate the controls, starting and stopping the flow of concrete at your command.

Most concrete trucks have only about 12 feet of chute on them. If the truck can't get within that distance of the foundation, you will have to plan on either wheeling the concrete by hand in the wheelbarrow to the foundation or making other provisions to unload the truck. As you are planning your material list, consider these factors in deciding whether to use transit-mixed concrete or to mix it yourself.

Substructure Materials

Once your foundation materials have been estimated, you have to figure the materials needed to build the substructure. This consists of posts, beams, joists, bridging, and the hardware to fasten them all together.

POSTS. To figure the number of posts necessary, you'll need to refer to the working drawings. Simply count the number of posts and record it on your material list. When figuring the number needed, be sure to check the elevation drawings to see the height of the posts. If your plans call for 5-foot high posts, order 10-footers and plan on cutting them in half.

If your plans call for placing the posts directly into the freshly poured concrete columns, don't forget to take into account the length of the post that will be embedded in the concrete. This should equal about $^2/_3$ of the depth of the column, but always leave at least 1 foot of solid concrete below the bottom of the post.

BEAMS. The beams can be either one solid piece of wood or they can be laminated. Laminated beams in general are stronger than a solid piece of wood. Unless you are buying the highest quality lumber available, without any knots (which is very expensive), the boards that you buy will have defects in them. At the location of these defects the board will be weaker. When you buy several smaller boards and fasten them together, it is unlikely that all the pieces will have a defect in exactly the same location.

As a chain is only as strong as its weakest link, a solid beam is only as strong as its weakest point. By fastening the boards together, the laminated piece ends up having several small weak spots instead of one larger weak spot. The links of the chain are stronger together, so to speak, making a laminated beam stronger than a solid one in most instances.

JOISTS. To estimate joists, simply refer to the working drawings. There will probably be a plan view showing the exact layout of the joists, unless the design is very basic. If the plan view shows the joist layout, you will merely have to count the number of joists shown.

If your set of plans doesn't include a plan view of the joist layout, it is not difficult to figure the joists. By keeping in mind a couple of basic rules, you shouldn't have any problems. First, record your information in such a way that you will understand it as you refer back to it when you start to build the deck. A sample worksheet form is included at the end of this chapter.

Say, for example, that your material list includes a 16-foot 2 x 10 that will be cut into a 10-foot piece and a 6-foot piece to be used as joists. Your material list also includes two 8-foot 2 x 10s to be used in a stairway. Three weeks later when you are just beginning to build the deck, you can't remember what the 16-foot piece was for. Your plans don't indicate any 16-foot pieces at all, so you know that it must be cut, but you don't know what it will be used for.

The only way to figure it out is to look back at the notes on your worksheet that you used to do the estimate. If you originally listed on the worksheet what the 16-foot piece is to be used for, you will not have a problem. If your notes were not organized, or if you threw them away, it may be more difficult to determine the use for this board.

The larger your deck, the more materials it will require, and the more of these types of incidents you will run into. Without organized notes, it can get quite confusing when the time comes to piece together your deck.

To figure the joists required if you don't have a plan view of them, first determine the direction that they will run. If your deck is 8' by 10', will you need 8-foot joists, or 10-foot ones? There will probably be more than one way to determine this from your plans.

One way would be to refer to the plan view that illustrates the deck's surface. Which way does the decking run? The joists will run perpendicular to the decking. Another way is to refer to an elevation or a section view of the deck. Either of these should show the length of the joists.

Once you have determined the length of the joists, you need to determine how far apart they will be spaced. This should also be noted on your plans in more than one location. To determine the number of joists, divide the width of the deck in feet by the spacing of the joists in feet, and add one.

You need to add one because the first one gets left out using this method. To illustrate this, pretend that your deck is 2 feet wide and the spacing is 2 feet on center. Two divided by two is one. But one joist would not be enough to build this deck. It would require two joists, one on each side.

For example, if your deck is 8 feet wide, and the spacing is 24 inches on center, divide 8 by 2, and add one. In this instance, you would need five joists. If your deck is 8 feet wide, and the spacing of the joists is 16 inches on center, you need to divide 8 by 1.33, and add one. You need seven joists.

When using this procedure, always round up to the nearest whole number. For instance, if your calculations showed that you needed 16.125 joists, round it up to 17 joists.

BRIDGING. To determine the necessary amount of bridging, refer to the plan view showing the layout of the joists. Bridging is the blocking that goes between the joists, tying them together into one unit. There are two types of bridging—solid blocking and strapping nailed in a crisscross pattern.

Generally, bridging is used if the joists span 8 or more feet. Use this rule of thumb if you are wondering whether you need bridging. In some instances it may not be necessary to buy materials for bridging. You might instead be able to use waste material.

Say, for example, that your plan called for 15-foot joists spaced 12 inches on center. If you will be using 16-foot pieces and cutting the extra foot off, this leftover piece could be used for the bridging. The more you utilize waste in this manner, the more money you will save.

HARDWARE. Estimating hardware is quite easy. It should, however, be done last. You simply need to count the places where connectors will be used on posts, beams, and joists and record their number on your material list.

Figuring nails is only slightly more difficult. Start by determining your planned nailing pattern. Once you've done this, determine how many nails it will take to fasten one board, then multiply by the number of boards you'll be using. This will give you the total number of nails you need.

Add 15 to 20% to this figure to cover for nails that

get bent or lost during construction, and to have a little extra. Next, refer to the table in Chapter 3 that lists approximate nail counts per pound. Use this to calculate how many pounds you'll need. Remember, when selecting nails the highest quality nails are the best value. Though their cost is quite a bit more than the ordinary nails, the extra amount of money required is very low when figured as a percentage of the overall deck cost. This little bit extra is well worth paying to ensure that the nails don't rust and cause unsightly stains on your deck.

Surface Materials

To estimate surface materials, use the plan view of your deck. It will list the overall dimensions of the deck. Determine the length of the decking pieces you will need. If this is an even number, say 16 feet, you merely have to figure how many it will take lying side by side to cover the width of the deck.

If this is an odd number, say 15 feet, you need to determine how you will arrive at this length. In order to avoid a seam in the decking, you may decide to order 16-foot pieces and cut off the extra foot that is not needed.

To save money and avoid waste, you may want to order 16-foot and 14-foot pieces. By cutting each in half, you would have two eights and two sevens. These could be used with each other to get the necessary 15 feet. You may decide to order all 10-foot pieces and cut some in half to give you 5-foot lengths. These could be used with the 10-foot piece to get the necessary length of 15 feet.

Whichever method you decide upon, be sure that the lengths you plan on using will be supported at both ends. Seams must land on a joist. You can't have a seam in between joists, as the decking boards are not strong enough. They would sag or break when stepped on.

Once you have determined the length of the decking, you need to figure the number of pieces to cover the entire surface. To do so, divide the overall width of the deck in inches by the actual width of the decking plus the space that will be between each piece. Use the chart in Chapter 2 that lists the actual sizes of lumber. This is much easier than it sounds, and it will give you the exact number of pieces that you need. Let's go through an example to understand it better. Suppose your deck will be 144 inches wide and 192 inches long. You will be using decking that is 16 feet long and has a nominal width of 6 inches.

The actual width of each board is only 5 1/2 inches. To this, you will add the space between boards, usually 1/4 inch (see Chapter 5 for information on spacing between boards). That equals 5 3/4 inches. Divide the overall width of the deck by that figure: 144 inches divided by 5.75 inches equals 25.04 pieces. Always round up to the nearest whole number. In this instance, you would need 26 pieces of decking 6 inches wide by 16 feet long.

There are several formulas that can be used to figure the decking, but they are not as accurate as this method, and usually call for you to add 10% extra as a safety factor to ensure that you have enough. This is not necessary and will cost you additional money. If you choose, you can order a piece or two extra to have in the event that one gets damaged during the construction process.

Stairs, Stringers, Trim, Fascia, and Other Lumber

The estimation of stair parts, railing parts, or any other element of the deck that is not part of the substructure or decking is primarily a matter of reading the plans to see what they call for. Rails may involve counting the number of balusters per foot and multiplying by the number of feet of railing.

ORDERING MATERIALS

Contractor Discounts

In some states (especially those that don't require licensing of contractors) and at some building supply outlets, you may be able to obtain the discount that is normally given to contractors. This usually ranges from 5 to 20%.

To get this discount may involve merely representing yourself as a contractor. If your state requires licensing of contractors, you may be asked to prove this by showing your license. If so, you will not be given the discount without one. However, in some areas of the country, you will qualify for the discount just by stating that you're a contractor.

In dealing with lumberyard personnel, it helps to have a general knowledge of lumberyard lingo and to appear knowledgeable. Knowing the contents of this book should be enough to satisfy the personnel at a lumberyard that you know what you are doing. Having a large lumber order is also very convincing. Even if you are not given the contractor discount, you will save money by ordering all your materials from a single supplier at one time.

Reducing Material Costs

It is possible to save hundreds of dollars by following these simple rules when you purchase construction materials:

1. GET COMPETITIVE BIDS. Once you have completed a detailed material list, get quotes from several lumberyards and building supply outlets in your area. The more bids you get, the more likely you are to find out who offers the best prices in your area.

2. DEAL WITH FIRMS THAT SPECIALIZE IN CONTRACTOR SALES. You may find that some of these will not sell to retail customers. However, many will. By going to these types of establishments, you will be dealing with outfits that are likely to offer the lowest prices. National chains are also likely to offer low prices because they buy in such large quantities and get big volume discounts for doing so. Some of this savings gets passed on to the customer.

3. ASK FOR THE BEST PRICE. Ask for each lumberyard's best price. Tell them that you are shopping around and will be purchasing the materials from the place that gives you the lowest bid. This will let them know that they are competing against other outlets and will give them an incentive to give you their best quote.

4. ORDER MATERIALS IN REGULARLY AVAILABLE SIZES AND GRADES. Nearly any size or grade that you want can be special-ordered; however, you will usually have to pay a substantial premium to do so. By using materials that are commonly stocked and available at lumberyards, you'll save money.

5. CONSOLIDATE YOUR PURCHASING. Let each lumberyard know, before they give you a quote, that you will be purchasing the materials all at once. This will save you money. The lumberyard can then plan on one delivery with a large truck, instead of several deliveries with a somewhat smaller truck. They will likely pass some of that savings on to you. Also, by purchasing all at once, you will be given volume discounts, saving even more.

If you plan on ordering all the materials at once, it is necessary to make provisions to store the materials until you are ready to use them. Keep in mind the distance to the job site. You will not want to store materials very far from the work area. It would be quite an additional amount of work if you have to hand-carry the materials 50 yards or more when it is time to use them.

Also keep in mind the damage to a lawn or garden that might occur as a result of storing materials on it for several weeks. The materials should be neatly stacked in a level spot, with stickers between each layer. This will prevent the materials from warping. They should also be covered with a waterproof material until they are used, to prevent shrinking and swelling.

MATERIAL LIST

	Qty.	Size	Description	Price Each	Total Cost
FOUNDATION:					
Sonotubes					
Cement					
Sand					
Crushed Stone					
SUBSTRUCTURE:					
Posts					
Beams					
Joists					
Decking					
Bracing					
Bridging					
Trim					
Fascia					
Stairs					
Railings					
HARDWARE:					
Nails					
Bolts					
Metal Connectors					
Post Attachments					
Miscellaneous					
FINISHES:					
Preservatives					
Stain					
Paint					

WORKSHEET

	Qty.	Size	Description
FOUNDATION:			
Concrete for footings	______	______	____________
	______	______	____________
Concrete for piers	______	______	____________
Materials for foundation forms	______	______	____________
	______	______	____________

Notes:

____

____

____

____

____

	Qty.	Size	Description
SUBSTRUCTURE:			
Posts	______	______	____________
	______	______	____________
Beams	______	______	____________
	______	______	____________
Joists	______	______	____________
	______	______	____________
Bridging	______	______	____________
	______	______	____________
Bracing—temporary	______	______	____________
Bracing—permanent	______	______	____________
Decking	______	______	____________
	______	______	____________

Notes:

____

____

____

____

____

	Qty.	Size	Description
STAIRS:			
Stringers	______	______	____________
	______	______	____________
Treads	______	______	____________
	______	______	____________
Risers	______	______	____________
	______	______	____________

Notes:

____

____

____

____

____

WORKSHEET, cont.

	Qty.	Size	Description
RAILINGS:			
Newel Posts			
Balusters			
Horizontal Railing			

Notes:

	Qty.	Size	Description
HARDWARE:			
Nails			
Bolts			
Metal Connectors			
Post Attachments			
Miscellaneous			

Notes:

	Qty.	Size	Description
FINISHES:			
Preservatives			
Stain			
Paint			

POINTS TO REMEMBER

- ❑ Estimate materials as accurately as possible, including concrete for the foundation, substructure materials, surface materials, and needs for stairs, trim, etc.
- ❑ Become familiar with lumberyard abbreviations.
- ❑ Find out about contractor discounts available to you.
- ❑ Reduce material costs by getting competitive bids, asking for the best price, ordering materials in typical sizes and grades, and consolidating purchasing.

5
Building a Simple Deck

Now that you're ready to start constructing your deck, study this chapter on basic deck-building techniques. It contains a wealth of guidelines for the novice carpenter. This chapter gives you complete instructions on how to build a simple deck from start to finish.

As you begin the construction phase, it is important to allow plenty of time to complete the project. As a novice, you will not be able to work as efficiently as a professional carpenter. If you are maintaining a full-time job, the amount of time that you'll be able to spend working on the deck is limited. The majority of it will probably be on weekends.

A job that would take a few days for a carpenter to complete will probably take you several weekends. You must be practical in your expectations before you attempt to start building the deck on your own. In so doing, you will shield yourself from the perception that the project is not getting accomplished in a satisfactory amount of time. By being realistic in your expectations, and by being persistent in your work on the deck, you will be rewarded with much satisfaction during and after the completion of your project.

GENERAL SAFETY PRECAUTIONS

In deck construction, not only is quality workmanship important, but safety is of the utmost concern. A proper knowledge of the tools used to build a deck, their functions, and the correct way to use them will help to ensure safety throughout the deck's construction process.

Dress

Always wear safety glasses when there is a potential threat to your eyes. This is especially true when sawing, nailing, and spray painting. You should also wear clothes that are appropriate for the job. Avoid clothes that are too tight or too loose. If clothes are too tight, they will restrict freedom of movement. Accidents are more likely to occur if your movement is restricted. If your clothing is too loose, it could get caught on something, such as a nail or saw blade.

You will probably work harder in clothing that you are not afraid to get dirty. Also, when you are wearing this clothing your mind will be free to focus entirely on the job. You will not be distracted from proper safety by being concerned with keeping your clothing clean.

You should remove anything that could be distracting such as wristwatches, rings, and other jewelry. Your shoes should have thick soles to protect your feet from protruding nails. It is also quite common in deck construction for boards and other objects to be dropped. Your shoes should have some type of protection against injury caused by falling objects.

Power Tools

Do not use any power tool until you understand it thoroughly. Any tool with a sharp edge for cutting can cause serious injury if used improperly. You should only use tools that are always sharp. If you attempt to use a tool that is dull, you will find that it is difficult to operate. It will require excessive force to make the tool perform its intended task.

If you have to use excessive force on a tool, you will not be in complete control. When you are straining to make a tool do its job, you are putting yourself in danger of an accident. When using sharp tools, you will find that they perform their job with ease. This allows you to be in complete control at all times.

To make adjustments or to change a blade of a power tool, turn it off and unplug its power supply. This rule must always be followed. It is extremely easy to press the on switch or pull a start trigger accidentally when making adjustments to tools. If this should happen with the tool still plugged in, serious injury could result. Many past injuries could have been avoided by this simple procedure.

Always pay attention to the tool when you are using it. Keep your eyes focused on the place where the cutting action is. Never try to use a tool and talk to someone at the same time. Also, whenever you use a tool, make sure that your fingers stay away from any moving cutting edges.

When you are finished using a tool, wait for the blade or cutter to come to a complete stop before you set it down. It is also important to unplug it before leaving to go on to the next task. This safety precaution is a good habit to develop. Store your tools in a safe place where there is no risk of tripping over the tool or of its falling onto someone (such as on top of a ladder).

Consideration should also be given to storing the tool in a place where it will not get damaged. You should only use tools that are in proper working condition. Never use a tool that is damaged or malfunctioning. Also, never use a power tool while you're in contact with water. If it is raining or drizzling, *do not use power tools*. Never use a power tool if any part of your body is in contact with moisture, such as standing on a wet lawn after a shower or early in the morning when the grass is covered with dew.

It is also important to ground power tools properly. Use three-prong extension cords plugged into three-prong electrical outlets. If these are not available, use a properly grounded three-to-two prong adapter. Consult an electrician if you have any doubts about the safety of your setup. Before plugging in any tool, make sure the switch is in the "off" position.

Other Safety Considerations

As you build your deck, you will often be required to lift heavy objects. When doing so, use the muscles in your legs. Do not lift heavy objects with your back muscles; this could result in serious back injury. To lift with proper form, bend your knees and get into a squatting position, keeping your back straight. Grasp or hold the object with both hands, and with your head upright and back straight, stand up.

Do not attempt to lift heavy objects by keeping your knees straight and bending at the waist. This is improper form. It is important, too, to have someone assist you when carrying long boards or materials. When you are working above another person, place materials such that they will not fall and cause injury.

Good safety involves good housekeeping habits. Materials and equipment should be stacked neatly. The work area should be cleaned often to keep it from becoming cluttered. Rubbish and scraps should be disposed of daily to reduce the risk of fire and accidents. Whenever you discover a protruding nail, remove it or bend it down immediately. If you don't, you will forget about it until you lean, sit, or step on it.

TOOLS

The basic tools you will need include: pencil, string, tape measure, utility knife, chalk line, nail apron, gloves, shovel, mason's hoe, wheelbarrow, framing and combination squares, level, hammer, nail set, pry bar, adjustable wrench, handsaw, safety glasses, power circular saw, power drill, drill bits, and sawhorses or a substitute for them.

DRAINAGE

The first step in constructing your deck is to make provisions for good drainage in the location where the deck will be placed. Low-level decks shade the sunshine from the area beneath them. Without good drainage, this area would always be wet, as the sun's rays would not evaporate the standing water. This water would tend to keep the underside of the deck constantly moist, thus speeding up the decaying process. It would also be a good breeding ground for mosquitoes and other insects.

A drainage ditch eliminates these problems. By keeping the ground dry, it also helps to stabilize the soil. If the soil were always wet, it would become unstable and the deck could possibly sink several inches.

Installing a drainage ditch is a simple procedure (see Figure 27). In sandy soils this is relatively easy, whereas in rocky soils a bit more labor is involved. Dig a trench from the lowest spot of the deck location to where the runoff will go. This trench should be at least 14 inches deep. Once this is completed, lay a 2-inch bed of crushed stone on the bottom of the trench. Any uniform size stone, from 3/4 to 3 inch, can be used.

Next, lay the drainage pipe in the trench. There are two common types used. One is a flexible plastic pipe with slots around the entire circumference of the pipe. It is usually black and is sold in coils of 250 feet. The other is a thin-walled 4-inch rigid PVC pipe. It is sold in 10-foot lengths. It has two rows of holes running the length of each section. If this kind is being used, place the holes so they are facing downward. By doing so, the groundwater will enter the pipe to be removed at a lower level than if the holes were placed facing upward. Once the pipe is installed, cover it with 6 inches of crushed stone. After this step is completed, cover the stone with a water-permeable shield. This shield, while allowing water to pass through it, will prevent fine particles of soil from washing down through the stone and clogging the drain pipe.

There is a product specifically made for this purpose. It is called Earth Felt and is relatively expensive. An inexpensive way to accomplish the same purpose is to cover the stone with a 2-inch layer of hay. This will cost much less but will be just as effective. The final step is to cover this layer with soil, filling the ditch to match the existing grade.

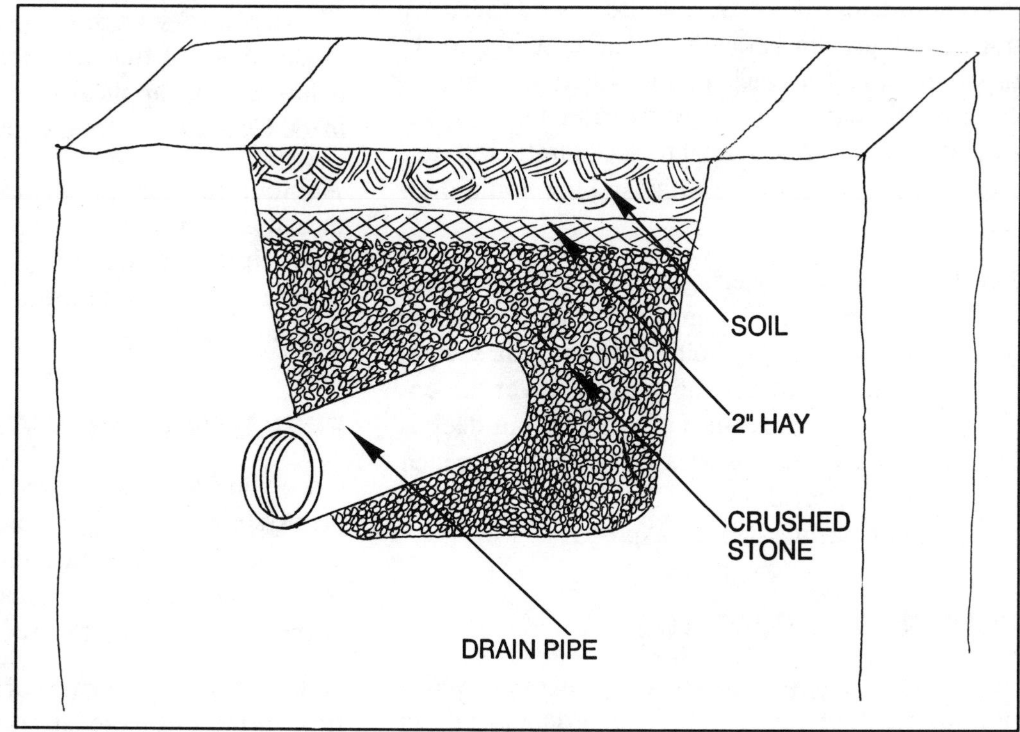

Figure 27. A cross-section of a drainage ditch.

EROSION AND WEED CONTROL

On a site with a steeper slope, such as a hillside, your concern will not be with drainage. Any rain or melted snow will automatically be removed due to the steeper slope. Of greater importance will be erosion. In extreme cases of erosion, soil could be washed away around and beneath the footings of your deck. It would then lose its structural integrity.

A common measure taken to prevent erosion is the installation of a bed of crushed stone in the area where runoff occurs. Typically, larger stones, from 3 to 6 inches, are used for this. In extreme cases, where the runoff is so great that it would wash away these stones, a bed of concrete is poured in the runoff channel. Once the concrete hardens, it will endure decades of running water.

Once measures have been taken to deal with drainage and erosion, you need to consider weed control. Although most low-level decks shield the ground beneath them from any sunlight, some weeds can still grow there. It is very unattractive to see weeds growing up between the boards on your deck's surface.

Before you actually start construction of the deck, it's best to take preventive steps to ensure there will not be any growth beneath it. The best way to do this is to install a black plastic sheeting. Whereas clear plastic will deteriorate if exposed over a period of time to direct sunlight, black plastic will not. It is specially designed to withstand the harmful effects of the sun.

Lay the plastic out, covering the entire area beneath the deck. To prevent it from blowing away on windy days, you will need to hold it down with several large rocks in various locations. Next, cover the entire plastic sheet with 1 inch of sand. If your deck is high enough so that this area is visible, bark mulch can be spread over the sand. This is much more appealing than leaving the sand exposed.

POURING THE FOOTINGS

The actual first step in constructing the deck itself is pouring the footings. Their location depends upon where posts are required. This was figured out when the working plans were drawn for your deck. It is necessary to locate the footings exactly as they are shown on the plan.

Footings must always be poured below the frost line. In northern states, this can be several feet below the earth's surface. A foundation pier is set on the footing and holds the posts. For most simple, low-level decks, the footing and pier can be poured at the same time. A common method for accomplishing this is the use of sonotubes (see Figure 28).

In areas where the ground freezes, it is essential that the walls of a foundation pier be smooth. This will allow the ground to travel freely up and down along the sides of the pier as it freezes and thaws. In most northern states, sonotubes are used for pouring the footing and pier in one unit. In southern states, footings are poured first, and precast piers are placed on the footings (see Figure 29).

FASTENING THE POSTS TO THE FOUNDATION

There are several methods for attaching the posts to the foundation. One method includes placing the posts directly into the freshly poured concrete and allowing it to set up. Only do this if the posts are made of wood that has been specially treated for below-ground applications. Pressure-treated wood in .80 CCA grade is one type.

Another method of fastening the posts to the foundation is the use of steel anchors that are placed directly into the freshly poured concrete. If you choose to use this method, be sure all the fasteners you purchase are galvanized.

PREPARING FOR INSTALLATION

Once you have determined the type of footing and pier system you will be using, you need to prepare the ground for their installation. To do so requires identifying their exact location. Batterboards are normally used to do this (see Figure 30).

Stake out the four corners of the deck as close as possible to their exact location, being sure that all four corners are square. A simple way to check square-

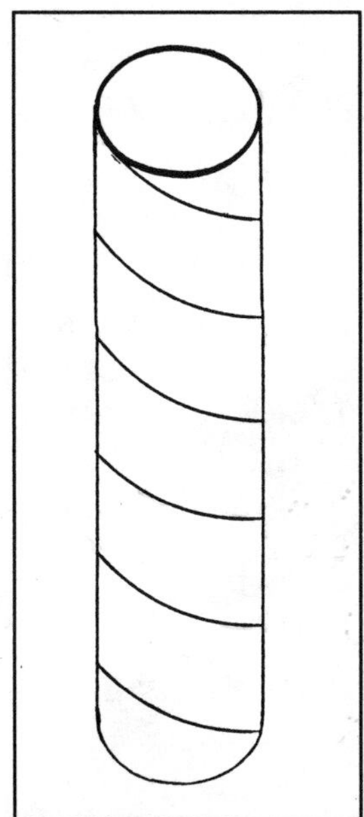

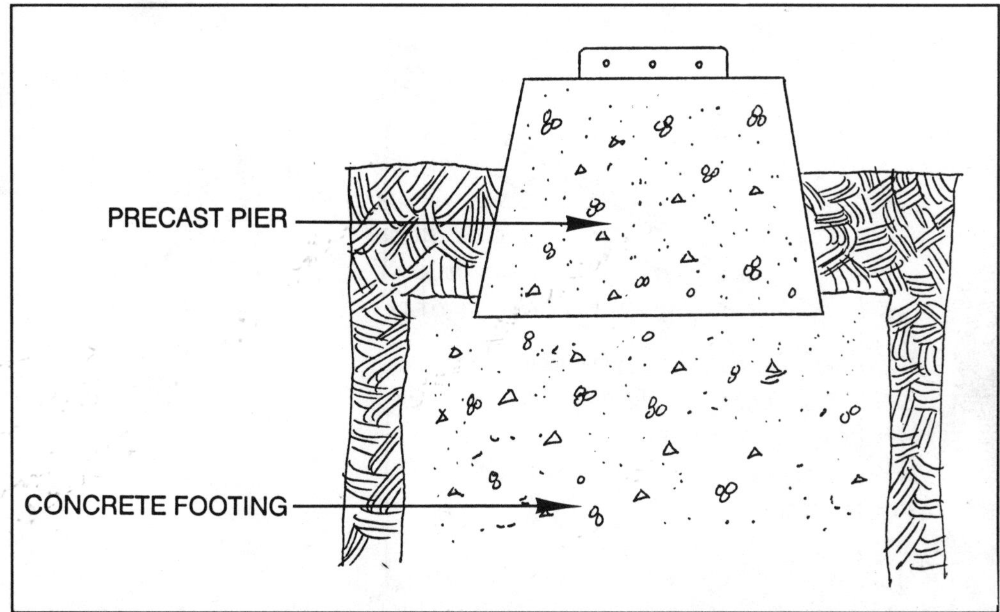

Figure 28. Left, strong cardboard forms, called Sonotubes, are often used for pouring concrete foundations for posts to rest upon. **Figure 29.** Right, a precast concrete pier permanently set on a concrete footing.

ness is to measure each diagonal (see Figure 31). If they are not the same, the layout is out of square. Continue to make modifications in the location of two corners on any side until the diagonals measure the same. This method works on squares as well as rectangles.

Once the locations of each of the four corners are marked by stakes, erect batterboards about 36 inches away from the corner (see Figure 30). This will give you enough room to dig holes for the footing and pier. At this point you need another person to assist you. Have your helper hold one end of the string so that it passes directly over one of the stakes and over the batterboard.

You should hold the other end of the string over the stake that is on the same side of the deck. Once this string is lined up properly over the stakes and batterboards, mark the location where the string passes over each batterboard. Now drive one nail into each batterboard where it has been marked. Do not pound the nail all the way in; leave about an inch showing.

Tie the string securely to one of these nails. Now pull the string taut and tie it securely to the other nail. In the same manner, you now need to install strings on the two sides that are perpendicular to the side just completed. However, this time you will not be holding the string over the stakes to find its location.

If you were to attempt to do it that way, it is likely that the corners of your deck would not be exactly 90°. Instead, you will use a procedure that guarantees your corners will be exactly square. It is the 3-4-5 triangulation method. A triangle with sides of this ratio will have an angle that is exactly 90°.

It does not matter whether this ratio is in inches, feet, or yards. It works in any measurement, as long as the ratio remains unchanged. To carry out this procedure, you'll need at least two tape measures and two assistants. The larger the triangle, the more accurate you are likely to be. Try to use at least a 6 by 8 by 10 foot triangle.

Start by holding the string over the two stakes that are perpendicular to the side that has already been done. Now mark the batterboard where the string crosses it. Drive a nail in the batterboard, leaving 1 inch exposed. Tie the string securely to the nail. Do not mark or fasten the other end of the string at this point.

From the point at which the strings cross, measure 6

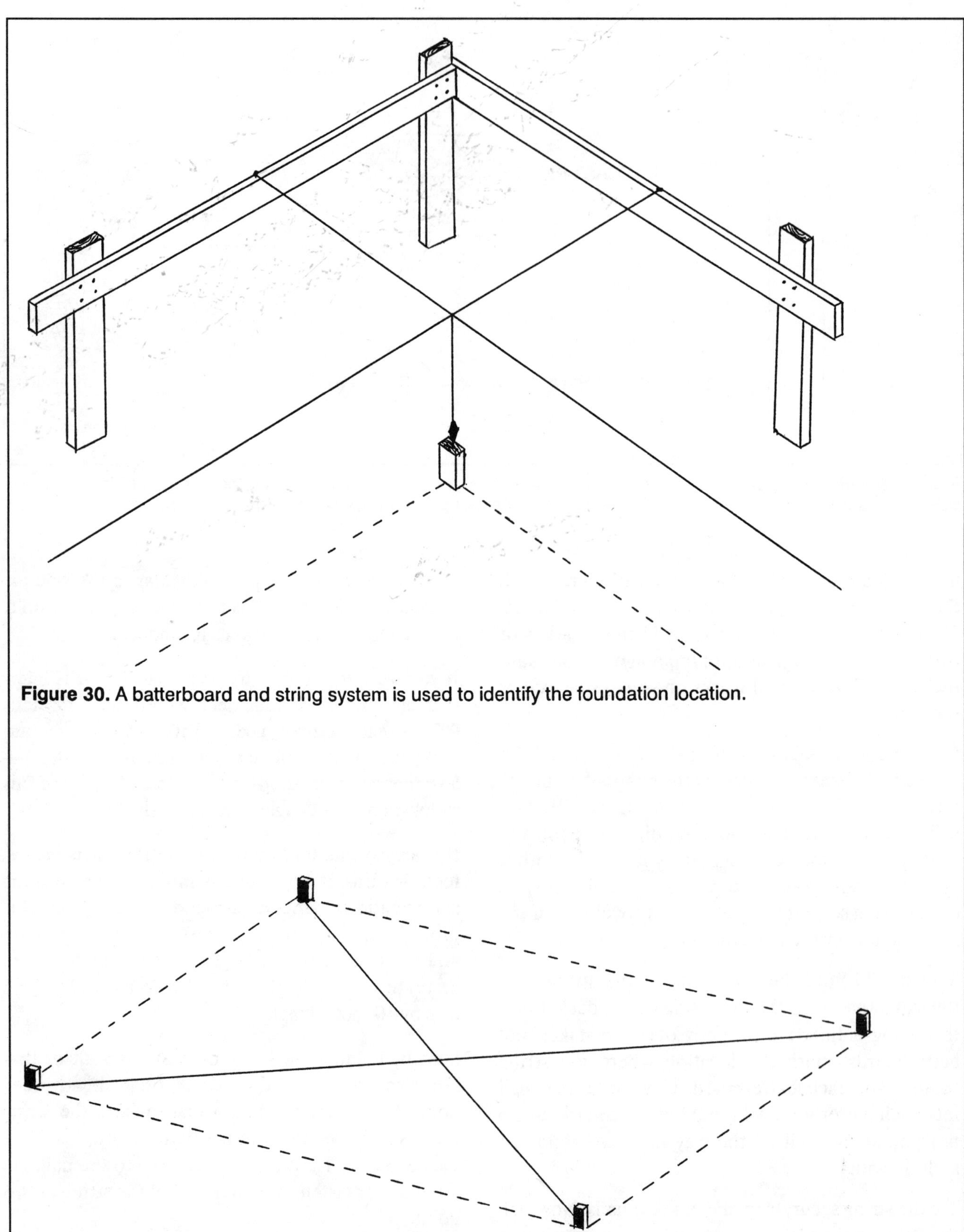

Figure 30. A batterboard and string system is used to identify the foundation location.

Figure 31. For perfect squareness, the diagonals should be equal.

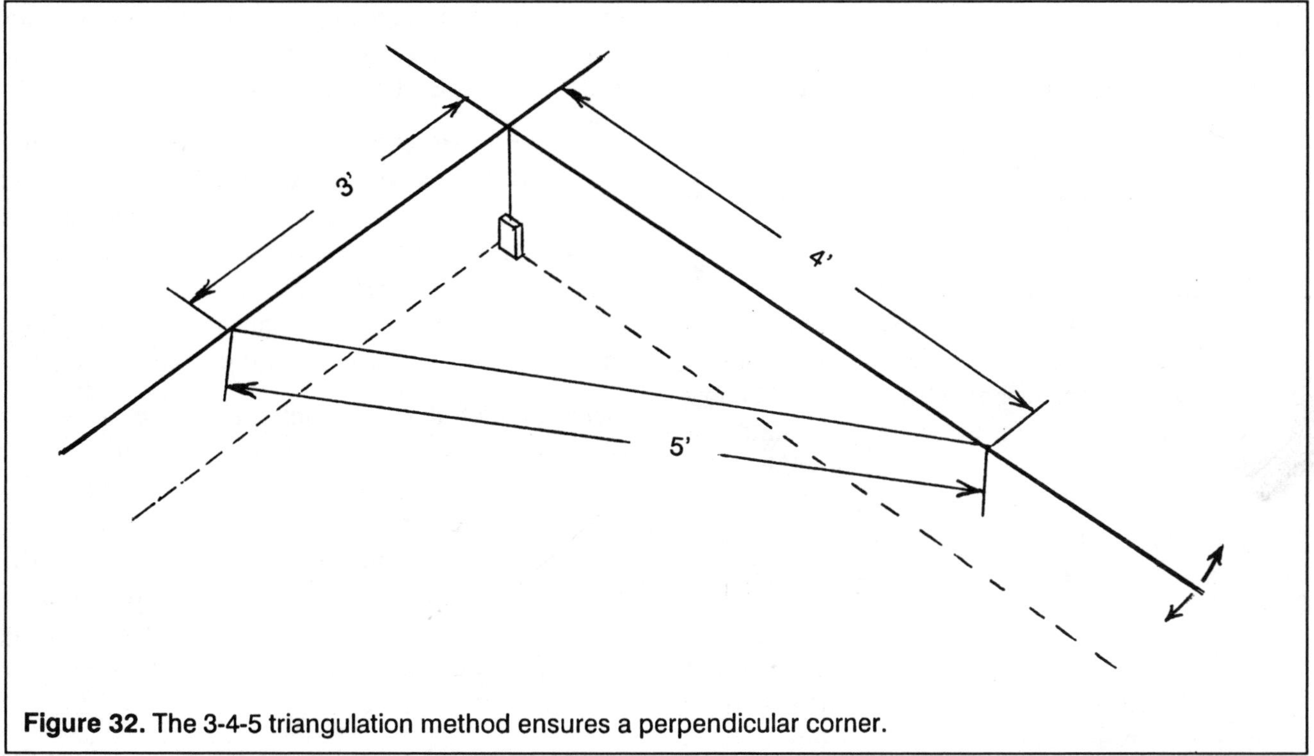

Figure 32. The 3-4-5 triangulation method ensures a perpendicular corner.

feet along one string, and 8 feet along the other. Move the string that has only one end secure sideways in whichever direction necessary, until the diagonal of this triangle measures exactly 10 feet (see Figure 32). Once this is accomplished, secure the string in this location by driving a nail in the batterboard, pulling the string taut, and tying it tightly to the nail.

The point where these strings cross is the location of the outside edge of one post. Check your plans to determine the locations of the remaining posts. Repeat the above procedure until strings have been installed on all sides. If you were exact in your measurements, the strings should form a square or rectangle that has perfect 90° corners. Check by measuring the diagonals. If they are not the same measurement, you may need to fine-tune the location of the strings.

You're now ready to start digging the holes for the footing. Use a plumb bob to plumb down from the corners where the strings cross to the ground. Remember that this is the location of the outside edge of the post and not its center. Now dig a hole for each post. The bottom of each hole should be at least 8 inches below the frost line. If you are using sonotubes, cut them so that when placed in the hole they'll extend about 6 inches above the ground.

POURING THE FOUNDATION

The first element to understand about foundations is the difference between cement and concrete. These two terms are not synonymous. Just as eggs are an ingredient in cake, so, too, is cement an ingredient in concrete. Just as eggs are not cake, neither is cement the same as concrete.

You will save yourself some embarrassment if you learn the difference between the two. Concrete consists of four ingredients: cement, sand, crushed stone, and water. The product is not concrete unless all four of these ingredients are present. The sand and crushed stone in this mixture are inert ingredients; the cement and water are active ingredients.

Cement is a gray powder that is made by burning lime and clay. A chemical reaction, called hydration, occurs when cement is mixed with water, causing the mixture to set up into a stone-like mass. This chemical reaction is what causes the cement to harden.

Depending on the amount of concrete required for your job, you may want to purchase aggregates that have been premixed. This ready-mix concrete is only lacking water. It is more convenient than mixing the ingredients yourself, but it is also more expensive. If your job requires only a small amount of concrete, the cost difference is minimal.

If you require a larger quantity of concrete, it is worthwhile to mix your own. You will need to purchase Portland cement, which comes in 94-pound bags. Each bag contains enough cement for 1 cubic foot of concrete. You must also purchase sand and crushed stone. Both must be specially washed for use in concrete mixtures. The sand should be coarse but not have particles larger than 1/4 inch. The crushed stone should be a uniform size, typically 3/4 or 1 inch.

If you purchase the cement before you are ready to use it, or if you do not use it all the same day, store it in a dry place. This will prevent lumps from forming. If the cement you are going to use has been exposed to moisture, don't use it unless the lumps can be pulverized by squeezing them in your hand.

In general, the water you use to mix the concrete must be clean and free from alkali, acid, or oil. A good rule to follow is only to use water that you would be able to drink. To determine how much concrete you need, see Chapter 4.

Mixing Concrete by Hand

Masons do their hand-mixing in a tub specially designed for that purpose. However, a wheelbarrow is adequate for your needs. You will need to measure the proportions of ingredients accurately. Strength, durability, wear resistance, and watertightness are controlled by proper proportions of the ingredients.

The American Concrete Institute has recommendations for the proportions of ingredients for many different applications and conditions. The following ratios apply to nearly all residential deck foundations: 1 part cement to 2 parts sand to 3 parts crushed stone.

To establish exact proportions, a bucket is sometimes used. For example, a batch of concrete could consist of 1/2 bucket of cement, 1 bucket of sand, and 1 1/2 buckets of crushed stone.

A proper mixture of concrete is thoroughly dry mixed before any water is added. Place the correct amounts of sand and cement in the wheelbarrow. Mix with a hoe until the mixture is uniform in color and appearance. Next, add the correct proportion of crushed stone. Stir with the hoe until it is uniformly distributed throughout the mixture.

Once completed, pull the mixture to one side of the wheelbarrow and add water. The amount of water to add will depend on the size of the mix and the wetness of the sand. If you were mixing an entire bag of cement in one batch, and were using dry sand, it would require about 5 gallons of water. If you were mixing a one-bag batch, and were using very wet sand, it would require only about 3 gallons of water.

Carefully work the dry mixture into the water at the bottom of the wheelbarrow a little at a time. If you were to attempt to mix the entire batch with water at once, it would require a tremendous amount of hard labor, and you would find it extremely difficult to do. By mixing the dry ingredients into the water, it will require a little less labor.

While you are mixing, be careful not to slop any of the mixture out of the wheelbarrow. The escaping water could weaken the mixture by carrying particles of cement with it. Continue until all the water has been mixed in. If the batch is too stiff when it is completed, add more water, a little at a time, and mix until the texture is right.

If the mix is too soupy, you will need to add more of the dry ingredients. It is important to dry-mix these in the right proportions before adding them to the wet mixture. You can do this in a bucket, and then mix in small amounts of this dry mixture until the consistency is right. When concrete is at this stage, small amounts of ingredients can make big differences in the texture.

You will find that hand-mixing concrete is very labor intensive. Jobs that require a large amount of mixing also require a great deal of endurance. To make your work easier, it is possible to rent an electrically powered concrete mixer from a local tool rental shop. The cost for this depends on the size of the mixer and the outlet that you rent it from. In general, expect the fee to be between $20 and $50 per day.

Whenever possible, concrete should be poured in one continuous pour. It is undesirable to have seams (called *cold joints* in the trade) in any footing or pier. If for some reason you need to have a joint, be sure to use reinforcing rods to fasten the two different pours together. These should be inserted in the concrete before it sets up. Leave at least 6 inches of the rods exposed, so that they will extend well into the second pour of concrete. This will strengthen the cold joint considerably.

In hot weather, protect the concrete from drying too rapidly. Try to keep it moist for a day or two after pouring. Spraying it lightly with a hose helps. Rapid drying will cause the concrete to lose some of its strength. In cold weather, it is necessary to protect the poured concrete from freezing. This can be done by laying insulation over it until it sets up.

After each footing or pier has been poured, spade or vibrate the concrete to force it into all parts of the forms. This will also remove any air pockets that would weaken the foundation. It is important to place the post, post anchor, or precast pier into the concrete immediately after you have finished doing this. By doing so the concrete will set up around the object and will ensure that a good bond is formed.

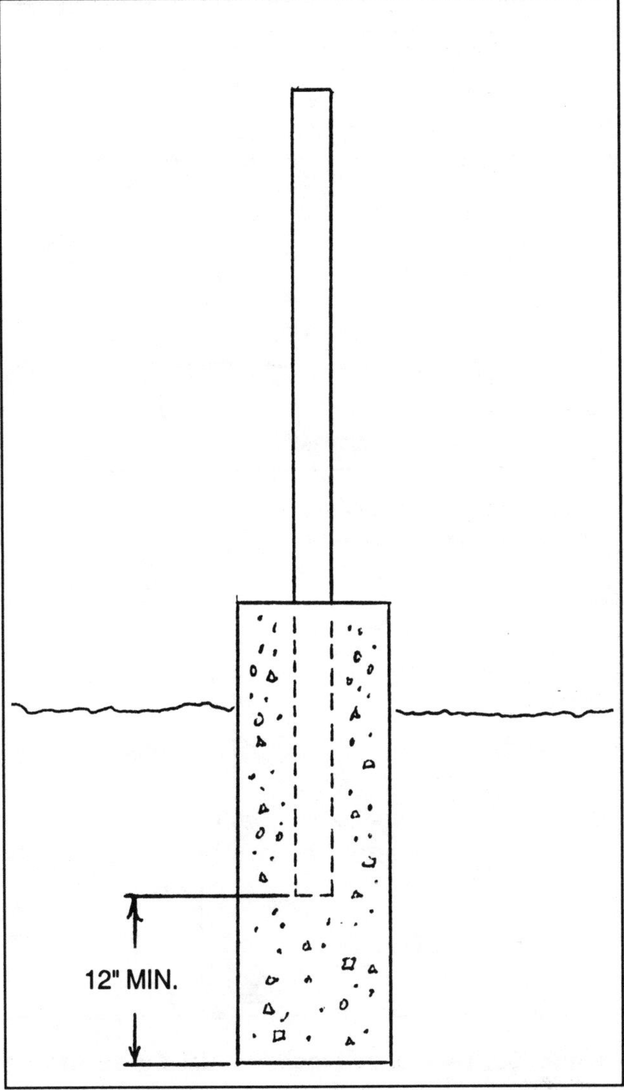

Figure 33. When placing posts in concrete, always leave a minimum of 12 inches of concrete below the bottom of the post.

If you are placing .80 CCA pressure-treated lumber into concrete that has been poured into a sonotube, be sure to leave at least 12 inches of concrete below the bottom of the post (see Figure 33). Remember, too, to plumb the post before leaving it. It is good to plumb each post twice: once when it is first set into the concrete, and once about one to two hours later. After a post has remained in the concrete for a while, some settling could occur. By checking it an hour or two after it is first installed, you will ensure that the concrete sets up with the post in a plumb position.

If precast piers are going to be used, the best method is to place them into the concrete footing before it sets up. Wet each one on the bottom before placing it in the concrete. Once the piers are in the proper location, level them in both directions.

If your footing has already hardened, it is necessary to place the pier in a bed of mortar on the footing. Mortar has the same ingredients as concrete, minus the crushed stone. Mix a small amount using the same directions as for concrete. Paste about 1/2 inch of mortar on the footing and on the pier. Position the pier on the footing and check to be sure the top is level.

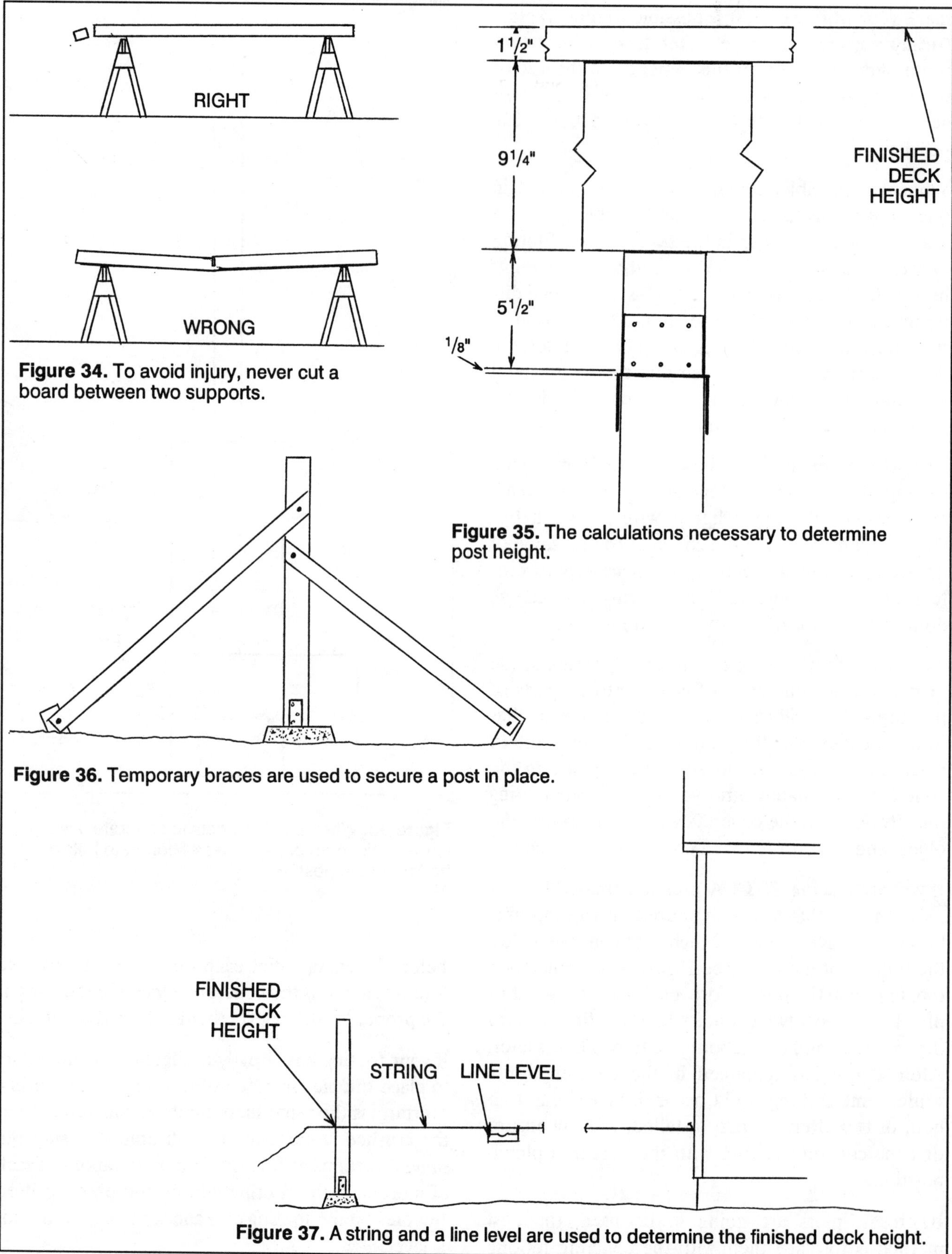

Figure 34. To avoid injury, never cut a board between two supports.

Figure 35. The calculations necessary to determine post height.

Figure 36. Temporary braces are used to secure a post in place.

Figure 37. A string and a line level are used to determine the finished deck height.

ERECTING POSTS AND BEAMS

At this point in construction, you will begin to assemble the wooden members of the deck. See Figure 34 for the proper method of cutting lumber. Proper procedures must be followed to ensure your safety. Use all guards on the tools properly, and never set a tool down until its blade or bit has stopped moving.

Before permanent installation of the posts is possible, you must determine post heights. To do so, you'll need to refer to your plans to determine the dimensions of the beams, joists, and decking that sit atop the posts.

The post height is equal to the finished height of the deck, minus the thickness of the decking, the width of the joists, the width of the beam, and the thickness of the metal post-to-beam connector if you will be using one (usually about 1/8 inch).

For example: Say your plans called for a 4 by 6 beam, 2 by 10 joists, 2 by 6 decking, and a metal post-to-beam connector. The post height would be 16 3/8 inches less than the finished deck height. This figure is arrived at by adding the thickness of the metal connector, 1/8 inch, plus the actual width of the beam, 5 1/2 inches, plus the actual width of the joists, 9 1/4 inches, plus the actual thickness of the decking, 1 1/2 inches (see Figure 35).

Before standing the first post in place, drive two boards into the ground approximately 3 feet from the footing (see Figure 36). These will be used to hold the post in place while you are measuring and building the deck. Place the first post on the foundation, and temporarily secure its position by attaching the two temporary braces to it with screws (see Figure 36). Using a drill with a screw tip in it will save time and make your job much easier.

The post must be plumb to measure it for the correct height. To plumb the post, you will need to loosen the screw that holds the brace to the post, but don't remove it entirely. While holding the level against the post with one hand, hold the drill in your other hand. Let the brace rest on the arm that is holding the level. Move the top of the post until it is in a plumb position. At that point, screw the brace back onto the post. Repeat this procedure for the other brace.

Once the post is plumb, you'll need to mark on it the finished height that is desired. To find this, either attach a nail on the wall of your house at the height that the deck will be, or have someone hold a string there. Pull the string taught and run it along the edge of the post. Hang a line level on the string, and move the string up or down until the line level indicates that the string is level (see Figure 37). Now mark that point on the post.

From this point, measure down the sum of the thickness of the decking, joists, beams, and metal connectors. This distance was previously figured. Mark this location on the post. This is where it will be cut. It is possible to cut the post in place if you are experienced in using a circular saw. If not, it is necessary to remove the post to cut it. For accuracy, make sure you use a square and mark all four sides of the post (see Figure 38).

Once the post is cut, it is possible to install it permanently on the foundation. Use the same temporary braces that were used to hold the post before. If you place the screws in the same hole, it should automatically position the post in a plumb position. Once the first post is in and plumb, set up each post, one at a time, to get their measurements for height.

To determine the height of the posts, it is not necessary to measure down from the finished deck's height. Simply use the string and go from the top of the first post over to each of the other posts. Pound a nail in the top of the first post, leaving 1 inch up. Tie the string to it and pound the remainder in. Using the string and the line level, come across to the second post. Mark the point at which the line is level. Do this to determine the height of the remaining posts.

Once the posts are all permanently installed and level, you are ready to install the beams that sit atop the posts. It is possible to use one solid piece of wood for the beams, but it is more common to build up the beams to the required size by fastening 2 by's together (see Figure 39). The boards are usually nailed together every 6 to 8 inches with 16d or 20d

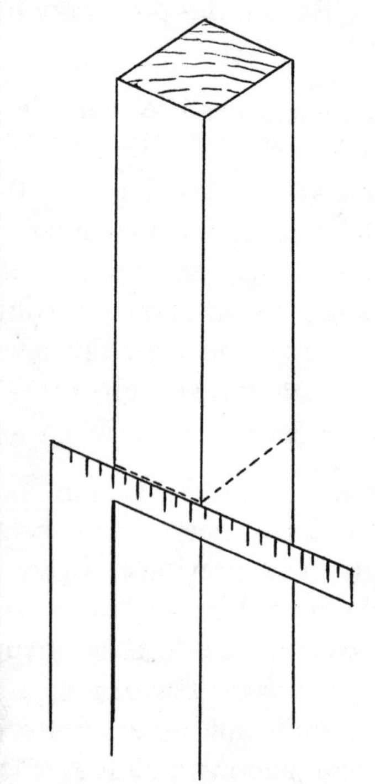

Figure 38. Use a framing square to mark all four sides of a post before cutting.

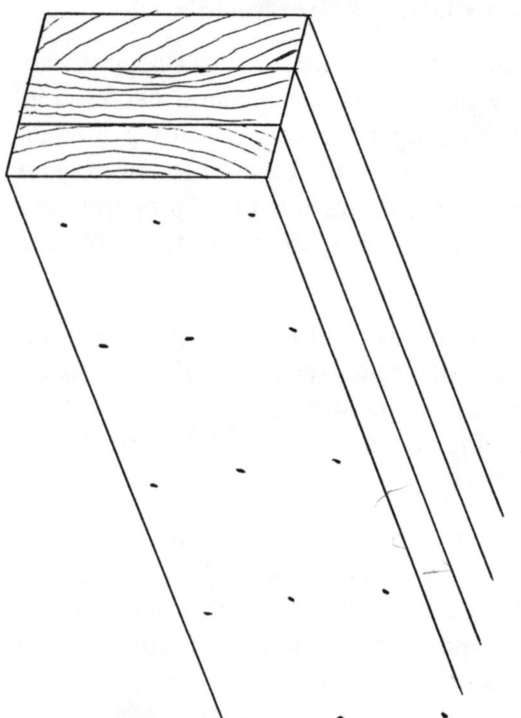

Figure 39. Three 2 x 10s are nailed together to make a beam.

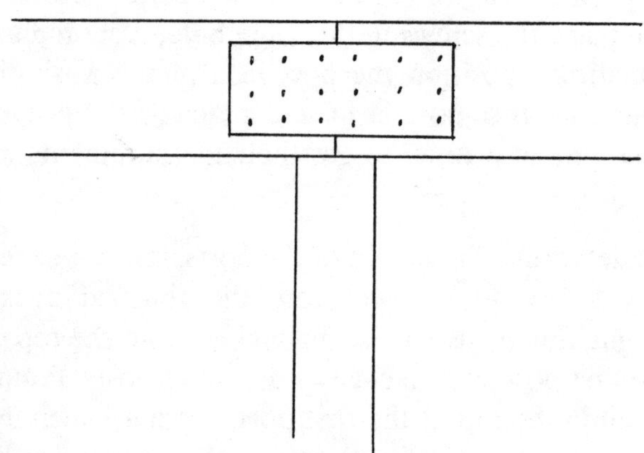

Figure 40. A gusset plate is used to connect two beams together.

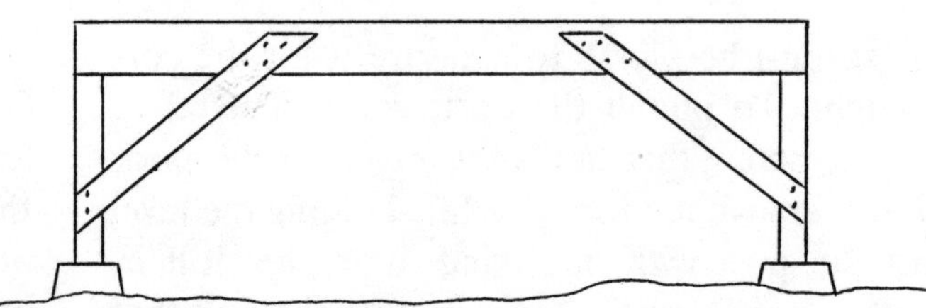

Figure 41. Diagonal bracing is used to strengthen the deck and to hold the posts in a plumb position.

nails, although some people prefer to bolt these boards together.

If you are building a long beam, it is important to stagger the seams of the boards. They should never be closer than 2 feet and preferably farther away than that. If two beams are to be joined together end to end, be sure that they both sit on a post, and use a gusset plate or strap to hold them together (see Figure 40).

If you are not using post-to-beam connectors, nail a board on the side of the post so that it sticks up past the top of the post by several inches. This will be used to hold the beam in place. You are now ready to set the beam in position. On low decks, this should not be a big problem. Nevertheless, lift the beam with your legs, and not with your back, setting it on the post. Tie this end of the beam to the metal connector or board before attempting to set the other end of the beam on a post. This will prevent the first end from falling off as the second end is lifted into place.

Once the beam is in position, check the posts to see if they are still plumb. It is quite possible that they moved slightly during the process of placing the beam. If they have moved, adjust them so they are again plumb. Now attach the beam to the posts. When the beam is secured, you will need to install braces to keep the posts plumb. Nail boards diagonally from the posts to the beam as shown in Figure 41. After this step is completed, you are ready to install the joists.

INSTALLING JOISTS

The board that the joists attach to is called a header, rim joist, or joist header (see Figure 42). This must be marked before you attempt to fasten the joists to it. Refer to your plans to determine the spacing of the joists. It is likely to be 16 or 24 inches on center, meaning the measurement from the center of one joist to the center of the one next to it. However, this is not true of the first two joists and the last two joists. They are closer together than the required spacing.

This is done on purpose so that the ends of lumber in standard lengths will fall on the center of joists. To mark out the header, place your tape measure on one end of it and mark the header at the spacing locations. These marks are the center of each joist. It is necessary to mark the edges in order to see the line while you are nailing the joist to the header.

If your spacing is 24 inches, and the thickness of your joist is 1 1/2 inches, you will need to mark the header at 23 1/4 inches and 24 3/4 inches. Using a square, draw a line across the header at these two locations. Continue doing this down the length of the header. In between these lines, mark a large X to show the location of the joists.

Once both headers are marked out, you will need to mark the joist's location on the top of the beams. To do so, use the same method that was used to mark the headers. Use a framing square to mark the edges of each joist. You are now ready to start putting the floor system together. To nail the header to the joists, nails are usually driven through the header and into the end grain of the joists. If your deck is close to the house, this may not be possible, and you will need to use metal joist hangers.

These joist hangers should be attached to the header before the joists are installed. However, they must be attached in the exact location that will make the top of the joist flush with the top of the header. To accomplish this, use a scrap piece that is the same size as the joist. If possible, cut this piece off a joist that is longer than it needs to be.

Lay the header down in a location where it will be easy to work with. Holding the block of wood so that it is flush with the top of the header, place a joist hanger on the block of wood and against the header. Nail one side of the joist hanger. The other side will not be nailed until the joist is placed in it. This will allow you to fine-tune the height of the joist hanger to ensure that each joist is at the correct height.

When all the joist hangers are attached using this method, you will be ready to start placing the joists on the beams. A method that I have found works well is to fasten the first and last joists to the two headers (see Figure 43). This unit is still relatively light and easy to work with.

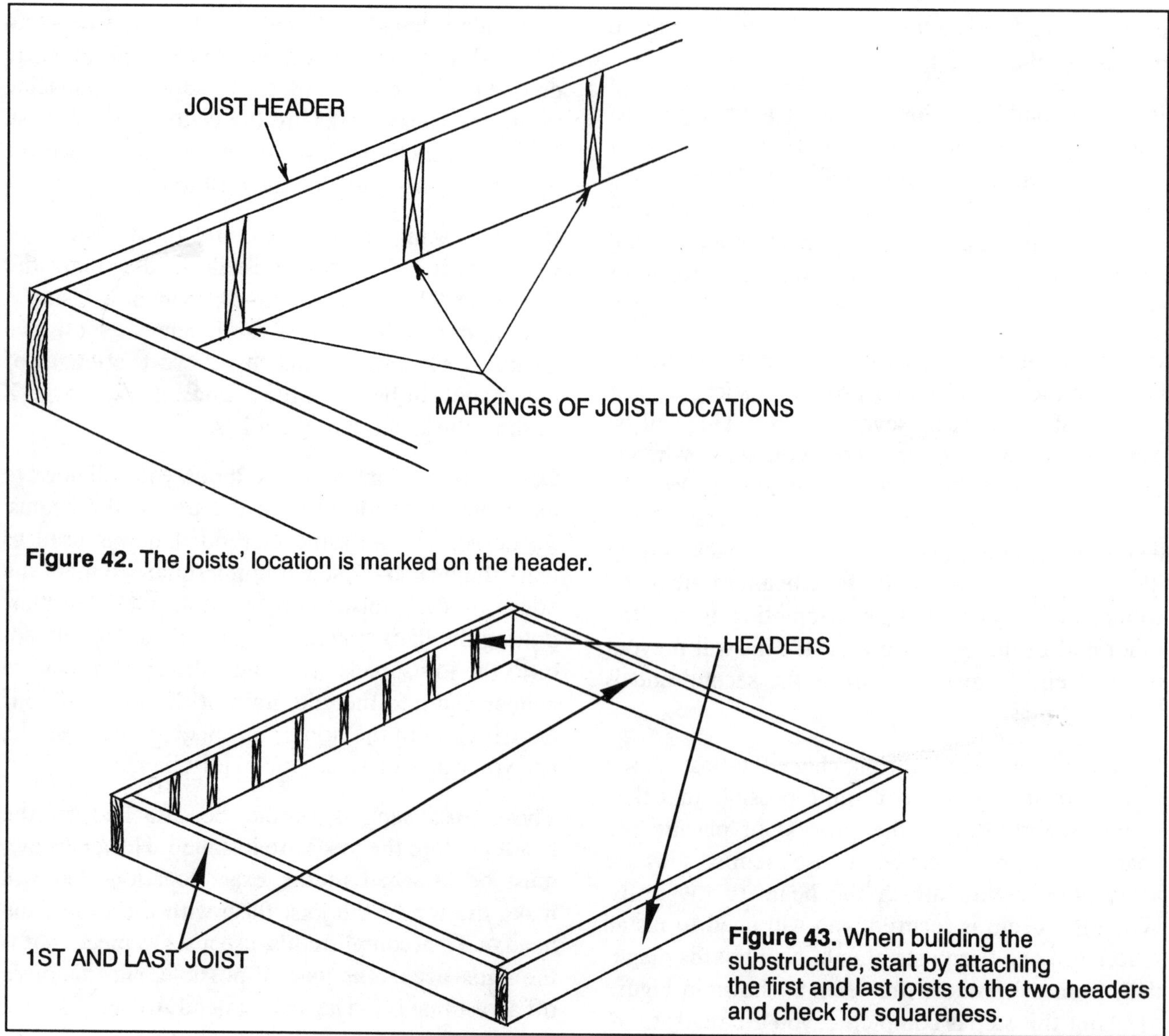

Figure 42. The joists' location is marked on the header.

Figure 43. When building the substructure, start by attaching the first and last joists to the two headers and check for squareness.

Lift this unit onto the beams and place it in the correct location. Before you nail it to the beams, check to see if it is square. A simple method is to measure the diagonals. If it is square, they will be the same. If it is out of square, nail one joist to the beams in the location that it needs to be. Once that is fastened, slide the other joist and headers until the diagonals are the same. Once accomplished, nail the second joist and the headers to the beams.

When this unit is fastened in place on the beams, it is simple to fill in the remainder of the joists. It's easier to fasten each joist as it is placed in its location, rather than place all the joists in and then try to secure them. The former method will give you more room to work as you nail the joists.

If your joists are longer than 8 feet, brace them by installing bridging. The two common methods for installing bridging are 1 by 3's nailed from the top of one joist to the bottom of another, or solid blocking (see Figure 44). The blocking is easier to install and stronger but costs slightly more.

Bridging not only keeps the joists from twisting when weight is placed on them, it transfers the weight from one to another, making the whole structure stronger. To install it, mark the center of the first and last joists. Snap a chalk line between these two marks. Using a framing square, go through and mark a vertical line down from the chalk line that is on top of each joist.

For joists that are 16 inches on center, the blocking will need to be 14 1/2 inches long, except for the first and last, which will need to be 13 3/4 inches long. For joists spaced 24 inches on center, the blocking will need to be 22 1/2 inches long, except for the first and last, which will need to be 21 3/4 inches long.

Nail the blocking between the joists, alternating from one side of the line to the other (see Figure 44). Check to be sure that the joists are staying straight. It may be necessary to trim a piece of blocking or two to keep the joists from bowing sideways. It is also important to be sure that the blocking is nailed tight to each joist. Ones that have already been nailed have a tendency to work their way loose as you are nailing the others.

When this step is finished, you'll be ready to install the decking. However, if you are going to be using a preservative and have chosen to coat your deck with it after it has been built, it is a good idea to coat the joists, posts, and beams at this stage. By doing it now, instead of waiting until the deck is complete, you will not have to climb under the deck later. (See Chapter 8 for information on deck preservatives and their application.)

INSTALLING THE DECKING

You will likely find that laying the wood decking is the easiest and most enjoyable part of building your deck. It is, however, also the most visible part of the deck, so you will not want to rush through it. Take your time to do a neat job. It will make a big difference in appearance.

For a uniform appearance, lay the decking boards so that the grain is the same on all of them. Boards will warp in the opposite way that the grain goes (see Figure 45). All decking boards must be supported on each end. If your deck is large and the decking boards will not reach from one end to the other, it is necessary to have seams where the end of one decking board butts against the end of another.

These seams must be on the center of joists. For appearance's sake, and also for structural integrity, do not line all the seams up on one or two joists. Instead, stagger them in a symmetrical manner as shown in Figure 46. By doing so, you will create a professional-looking job.

The decking boards must have a space between them to provide for proper drainage and air circulation for drying. The recommended spacing is 1/4 inch. It will save time to use spacers as you are nailing the decking. Cut boards of the desired thickness about 6 inches long. Plywood lends itself well for this purpose.

Once the first decking board has been nailed in place, position three of these spacers next to the first piece of decking so that they butt against it and rest on a joist. Place one at each end and one in the middle. Slide the next decking board into place and hold it firmly against these spacers. This will automatically position the board, ensuring the proper space is maintained. This method also guarantees that all the spacing will be uniform.

It is better to start closest to the house and work out from there. By so doing, the installation of the last few decking boards will be easier, as there will be sufficient room to work out away from the house. This will also ensure that the decking board closest to the house is parallel to it, and you'll be able to position it as near to or as far from the house as you desire. Ideally, it is best to leave at least a 1-inch space to allow water and snow melt to drain off the deck.

Hand-nailing gives the neatest possible job. To get a professional look, pound the nails into the wood until the heads are about 1/16 to 1/8 inch above the surface. When all the decking is secured in this manner, use a nail set to drive the heads so they are just below the surface of the wood. This will eliminate any indentations caused by the hammer hitting the decking boards.

The decking should be nailed at every point that it contacts a joist. Nails should be driven in perpendicular to the decking, except where two pieces of decking end on one joist. In this instance only, you should drive the nails through the decking and into the joist at approximately a 30° angle (see Figure 47).

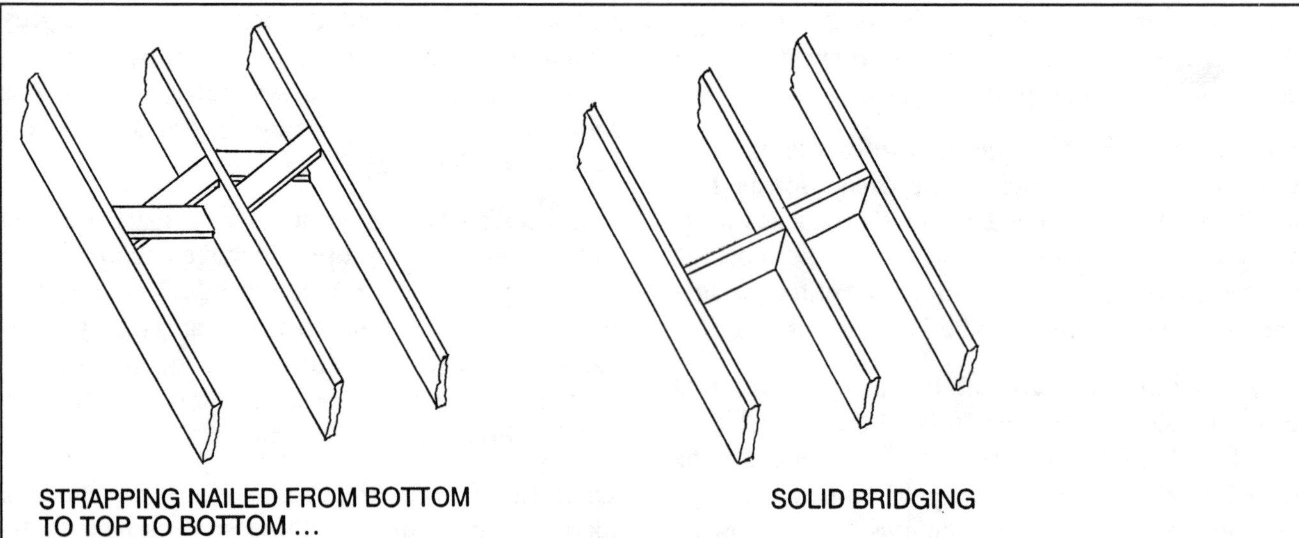

Figure 44. Two common methods of installing bridging.

Figure 45. Install the decking boards so that the grain faces the same way on each piece.

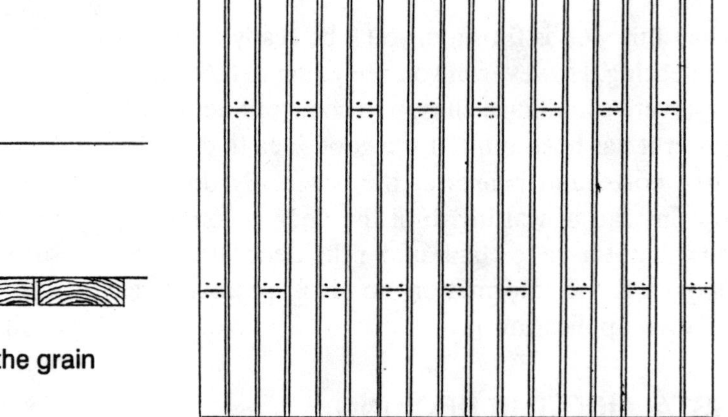

Figure 46. If the decking boards are not long enough to reach from one edge of the deck to the other, stagger the seams in a symmetrical manner.

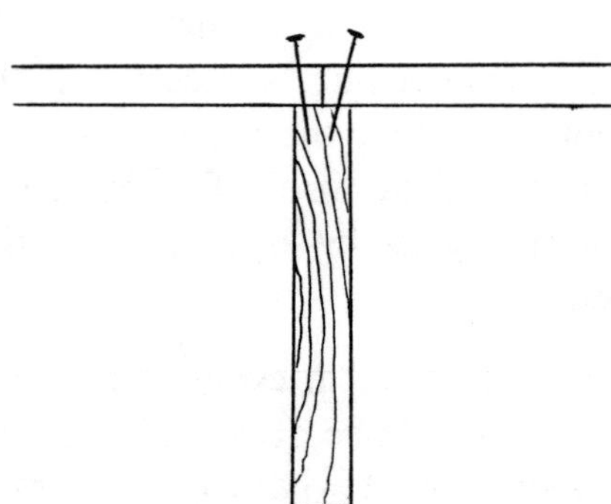

Figure 47. When two decking boards meet, drive the nails in at approximately a 30° angle.

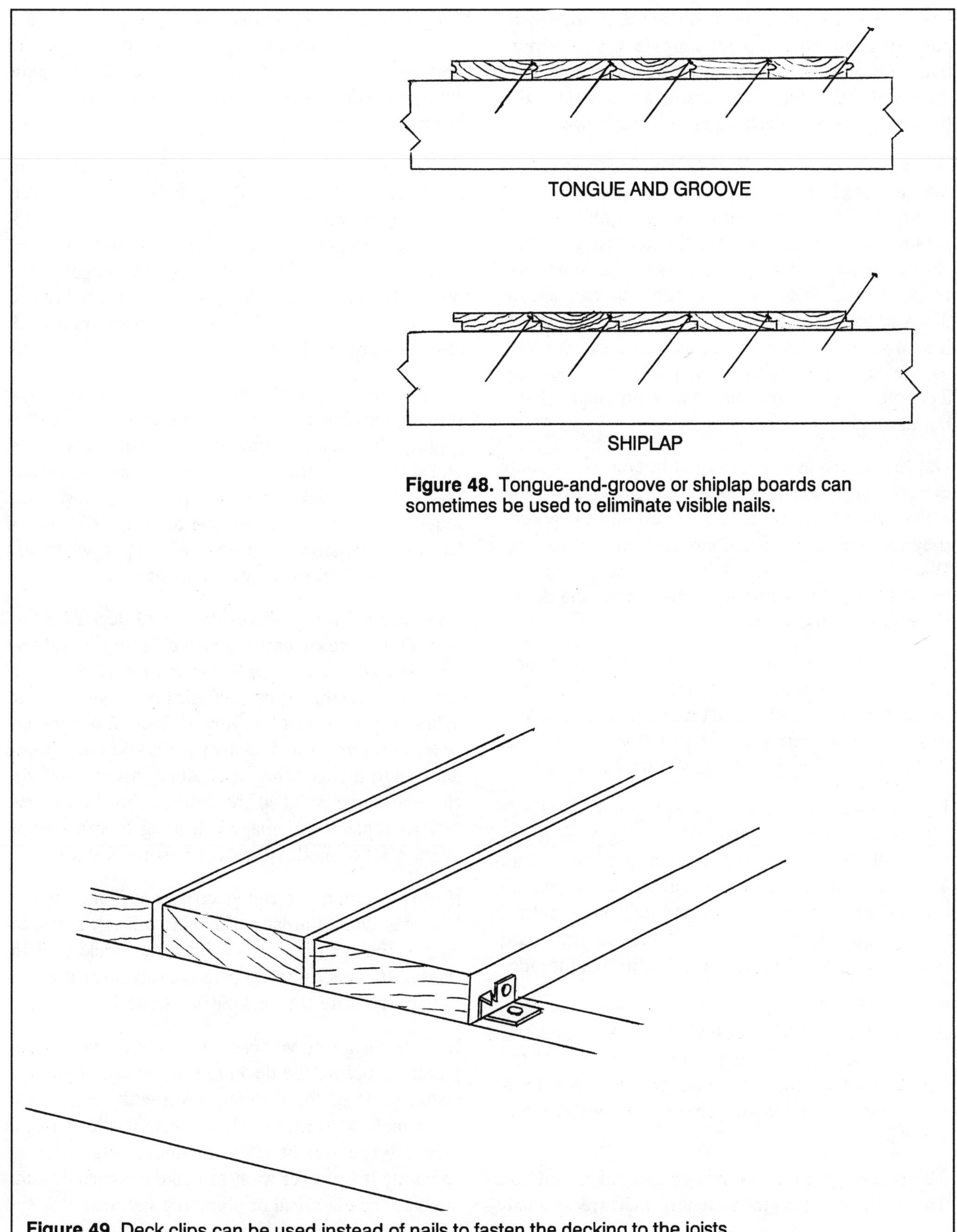

Figure 48. Tongue-and-groove or shiplap boards can sometimes be used to eliminate visible nails.

Figure 49. Deck clips can be used instead of nails to fasten the decking to the joists.

Unless you are planning to fill the nail holes with putty or caulking and paint your deck, it is important to locate the nails in each board so that they form a straight line. This arrangement looks quite tidy and gives your deck a quality appearance.

When nailing near the ends of boards, you may find that they split rather easily. This is especially true of redwood and western red cedar. Two methods are commonly used to overcome this tendency to split. A simple method carpenters use is to blunt the point of each nail. To do so, turn the nail upside down so the point is facing up. With the head resting on something hard, such as a rock or concrete, use your hammer to tap on the point gently. Do this a couple of times until the point is no longer sharp, but flattened.

Use these nails near the ends of boards where there is a greater tendency to split. The reason this works is that when sharp points are driven into the boards they separate the wood fibers and cause it to split. When the point is blunted, instead of separating the wood fibers, the flat spot crushes them and drives them through the wood.

Nails that have had their points blunted tend to predrill their own hole as they are going through the wood. If this method doesn't work, it is necessary to drill pilot holes with a power drill. Choose a drill bit that is about 3/4 the size of the shank of your nail.

For the ultimate in sleek deck appearance, it is possible to fasten the decking without any nails showing at all. There are three methods used to do this. The first is to use a tongue-and-groove or shiplap board (see Figure 48). These are "blind nailed" through the edges of each board and the next board is placed tight to it, hiding the nails through the side.

Wood swells and shrinks as it gets wet and dries, making this method undesirable for wood decks. It can be used, however, if you live in an area of the country that is rather dry, and if you use a good water sealer to reduce the amount of swelling and shrinking.

The second method involves the use of deck clips. These are small metal fasteners that are specially designed to attach the decking to the joist invisibly. They are nailed to the edge of each decking board and also to the joist. There is a special metal tongue that protrudes away from the edge of the decking board.

When the next board is installed, it is driven toward the board that has already been fastened, and this tongue penetrates the edge of the board. This holds the board in place on that side, and another set of decking clips is used on the opposite edge of the board. In this manner, both sides of the board are held in place by the clips. Figure 49 shows a deck clip nailed properly in place.

Keep in mind, though, that each deck clip costs approximately fourteen cents, compared to a cost of slightly less than a penny for each nail. This would add about $40 to the cost of a small deck. This really isn't a substantial difference, but it will also take much more time to install the decking. The added labor and expense are probably worth it, when you consider the improvement in appearance.

The third method involves the use of decking adhesive. This comes in cartridges that fit into a caulking gun. The adhesive is applied to the top of the joists, and the decking is pressed firmly down onto it. When it sets up, it will be very difficult, if not impossible, to remove the decking boards without causing damage to them or the joists. Keep this in mind, because at some point in the future it may be necessary to replace a damaged decking board, or you might want to modify the deck in some fashion.

If you're planning to run electricity or plumbing to a low-level deck, the lack of height will not allow access to the area beneath it once the decking is installed. It is necessary to take measures for their installation before the decking is installed.

In these instances, you can either run the wiring and plumbing before the decking is installed, or you can fasten some of the decking down with screws. The latter method is preferable because it allows future access to the area beneath the deck. This will come in handy if you ever want to make changes or additions to the electrical or plumbing systems.

How to Straighten a Bowed Decking Board

As you are nailing the decking boards, you'll discover that not all boards are perfectly straight. This can cause a couple of problems: one is that your decking may wander somewhat from being parallel. It is important to check often as you are installing the decking to see if this is occurring.

A simple method for checking is to measure the distance from the edge of the rim joist to the edge of the decking being installed. Do this at both ends of the deck. As long as both measurements are the same, the decking is remaining parallel. If the measurements are different, you will need to compensate by adding about 1/16 inch to the space between decking boards on one end, until the measurements are the same. If this step is not taken, the deck will end up with an uneven overhang.

Some boards may be bowed in the middle. To keep the decking parallel and the gap between each board even for the entire length of each piece, it is necessary to straighten it. To correct the problem, nail the board to the joists on both ends. Next, nail a scrap piece of 2 by 6 parallel to the decking board, leaving about a 3/4-inch gap between the two.

You'll now need assistance from another person. Place a pry-bar between the 2 by 6 and the bowed decking board. Pry the board into place. While you are holding the board, your helper should nail it. Do not release tension on the pry-bar until all the nails have been pounded in. If you release it before then, the board will likely spring back out of place or possibly even split.

Cutting the Decking

After all the decking has been installed, you should cut it to get a perfectly straight edge on your deck. This means that the decking should extend over the edge enough so that the excess can be trimmed upon completion.

If you have developed skill with the circular saw, you can snap a chalkline and cut the decking "freehand." If you can't use a circular saw like a pro, you can still get the same results. Tack a board onto the decking at an appropriate place for your saw to slide along as you are cutting. This guide will ensure that a straight line is made by the passing saw.

POINTS TO REMEMBER

- ❑ Take safety precautions seriously. Dress properly, use power tools carefully, use proper form for lifting heavy objects, and keep the work area neat.
- ❑ Provide good drainage.
- ❑ Allow for erosion and weed control.
- ❑ Become familiar with basic deck-building steps and follow them carefully.

6
Advanced Deck-Building Techniques

If you feel adventurous and would like to attempt the construction of a more advanced deck design, this chapter will help. It contains tips and instructions on building stairs, railings, benches, and overheads.

STAIRS

Stair Parts and Terms

Before delving into the design and construction aspects of stairs, you need to familiarize yourself with a few common stair parts and terms. These include stringer, rise, run, riser, tread, winder, nosing, newel, baluster, handrail, platform, landing, total rise, and total run.

STRINGER — (See Figure 51.) The main board that supports the treads, the risers, and the load placed on the stairway by people and objects. There are three common kinds of stringers: cleat, built-up, and cutout. These are discussed later in this section.

RISE—The total vertical distance from one step to the next (see Figure 51).

RUN—The total horizontal distance from the edge of one tread to the edge of the next (see Figure 51).

RISER—The term used for the board that is nailed on the vertical face of one step (see Figure 51).

TREAD—The board that goes on the horizontal face of the step. It is the piece that one steps on while climbing up a stairway (see Figure 51).

WINDER—A wedge-shaped tread located in the part of a stairway that turns (see Figure 52).

NOSING—The projection of a tread beyond the front edge of the riser (see Figure 53).

NEWEL—The main post at the start of a railing, or the larger post that stiffens the railing where it comes together at an angle such as at a platform. This is also referred to as a newel post (see Figure 54).

BALUSTERS—The vertical members that support the railing. They are smaller than the newel and not as strong, but protect children from falling off the edge of the stairs (see Figure 54).

HANDRAIL—The top piece on a railing that is grasped and held onto for support as one goes up or down the stairs (see Figure 54).

PLATFORM—A flat, level, intermediate area between two parts of a flight of stairs (see Figure 55).

LANDING—The floor at the top or bottom of stairs where they begin or end. This term is also occasionally used to describe a platform (see Figure 55).

TOTAL RISE—The total vertical distance from the bottom to the top of the stairs. For instance, the total rise would be from the ground to the top of the decking, or from the top of the decking on one level to the top of the decking on a different level (see Figure 56).

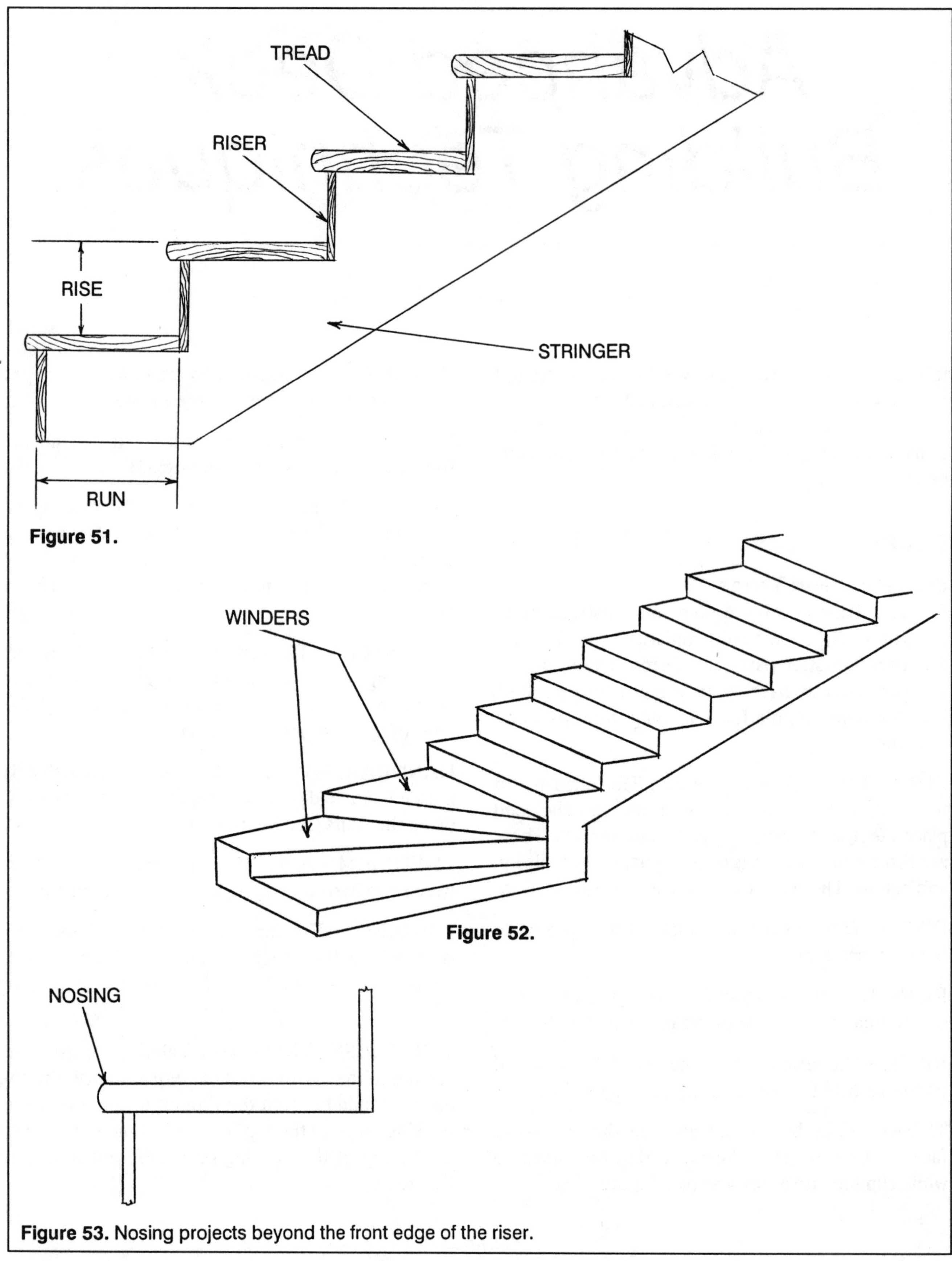

Figure 51.

Figure 52.

Figure 53. Nosing projects beyond the front edge of the riser.

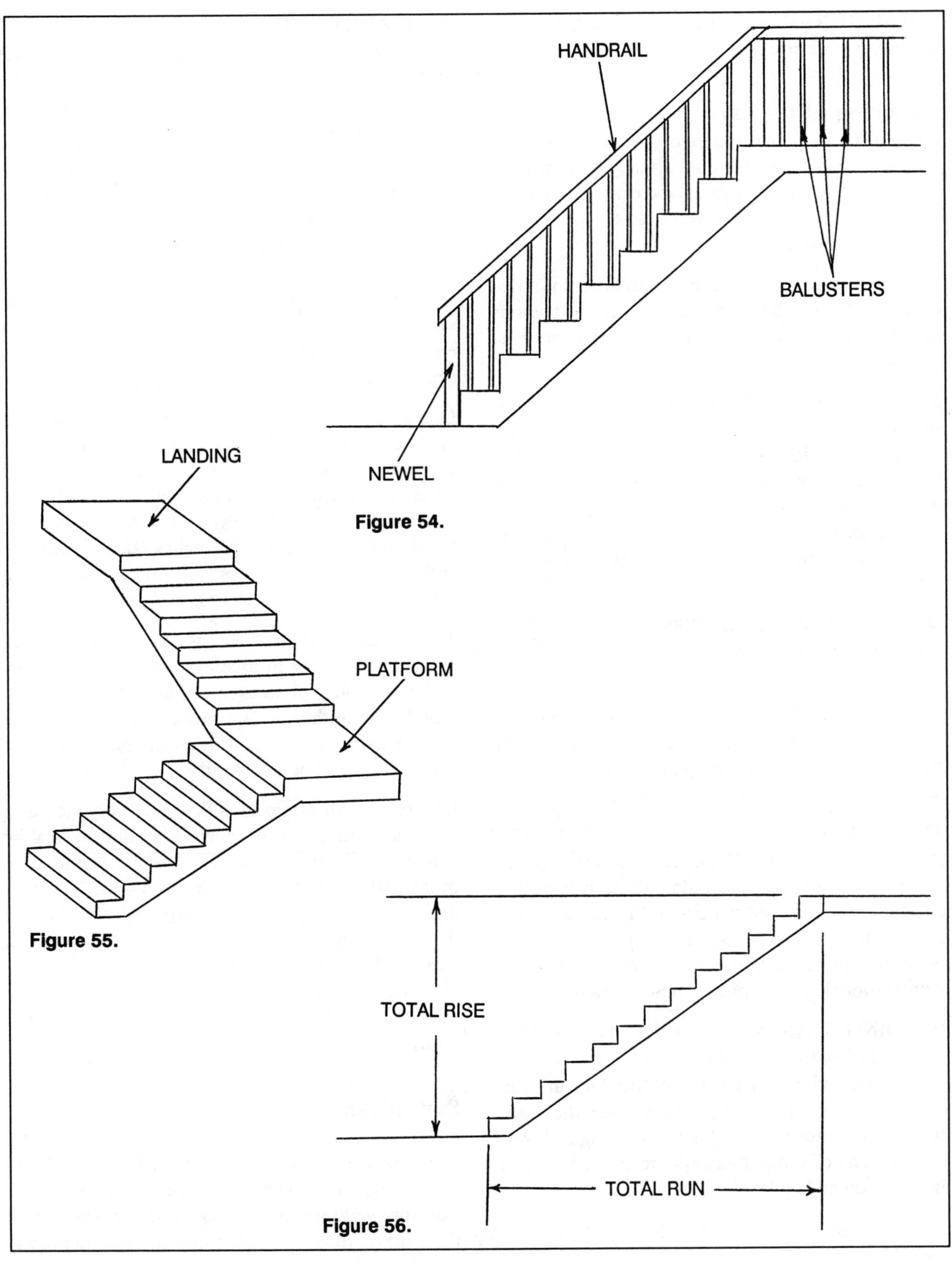

Figure 54.

Figure 55.

Figure 56.

TOTAL RUN—The total horizontal length of the stairway (see Figure 56).

Designing a Stairway

If you hired someone to design your deck and draw the plans, the stairway should already be designed. However, if you are designing and drawing the deck plans yourself, there are several factors to consider as you design stairways.

The first element to consider is the different styles to choose from. There are three general categories to choose from: straight run stairs, stairs with landings, and winding stairways.

Other important considerations in the stairway's design include the width of the stairs, the relationship between the height of the riser and the width of the tread, which combined will determine how steep the stairway is, and the arrangement. Safety, and to a lesser degree convenience, are the primary factors to consider as these elements are decided upon.

Different Types of Stairways

The three basic categories and their uses are as follows:

STRAIGHT RUN. This stairway is the simplest in design and is the easiest to build; however, it will still be rather difficult for someone who does not have any experience in building stairways.

STAIRWAYS WITH PLATFORMS OR LANDINGS. These can be U-shaped, L-shaped, or T-shaped. They are somewhat more difficult to design and build but will add variety and elegance to the appearance of your deck. If you have very little building experience, you may need the assistance of a professional to build one of these stairways.

WINDING STAIRWAYS. By far, these are the most complex to build and design. Unless you are very handy and have good geometric skills in dealing with angles, you will probably need the assistance of a professional to build a winding stairway. The designs of these stairways are limited only by imagination and budget.

Riser and Tread Relationship

It is important to consider your own individual preference and circumstances as you determine the height of the rise and the width of the tread. There are some guidelines to follow, however.

Code requirements vary, but in general the rise is limited to 7 or 7½ inches. The tread requirements usually call for a width of at least 9 inches. In general, older people prefer a smaller rise than younger people, and, if teenagers had their way, a rise that is larger than code permits would be used. There are several formulas used by architects and designers to ensure that tread to riser ratios remain within acceptable limits.

One such formula is that the sum of one riser and one tread should equal between 17 and 18 inches. For instance, according to this formula, if you chose a riser of 7 inches, you should choose a tread width of 10 or 11 inches. If the riser will be 5 inches, the tread should be 12 or 13 inches. If you were to choose a riser of 4 inches, the formula suggests a tread width of 13 or 14 inches.

The reason for this formula is to keep the amount of stride necessary to ascend or descend the stairs within the range of an average adult in healthy condition. The author has no problem whatsoever designing stairs that are outside of the boundaries set forth by this and other formulas.

One reason for doing so is that not everyone has a stride matching that of an average adult in healthy condition. For any number of reasons (such as knee problems), your stride may be different. You may desire a rise of only 4 inches coupled with a tread that is 11 inches wide. If that is what you desire, build it that way. The formulas are only guidelines, not cast-in-stone rules that must be followed. Be sure that your design meets code requirements, though.

Stair Width

Stairs must be wide enough for two people to pass on them. The absolute minimum is 36 inches. However, making them wider than that is recommended. Consider *what* will be passing on the stairway. Will there need to be enough room for two people to carry a portable grill on it? What about deck furniture? Will that have to be carried up and down the stairway? Try to build the stairway wide enough so that nearly anything can pass on it.

Laying Out a Stairway

As you are considering the size of the tread and riser, take into account the total rise of the stairway. The quotient of total rise divided by the rise must be a whole number. That is because the total rise divided by the rise is the number of steps that will be in your stairway. You cannot have fractions of steps.

If you do not choose a rise that divides evenly into the total rise without a remaining fraction, you will end up with one rise that is different from all the others. Let's go through an example. If the total rise is 62 1/2 inches, and you desire a rise of 6 1/2 inches, divide 62 1/2 by 6 1/2 to get an answer of 9.61 stairs. You must decide whether you want to raise or lower the rise.

If you desire a smaller rise, round the 9.61 stairs up to 10. Now divide the total run, 62 1/2 inches, by the number of stairs, ten. The answer is that each rise should be 6 1/4 inches. Once you have determined the number of stairs in this manner, you will be able to figure the total run. To do so, multiply the number of stairs, minus one, by the tread width.

You need to subtract one because the top rise will lead to the next level, and it does not have a tread. In the above example, if the tread width is 11 inches, the total run would be 9 x 11, or 99 inches. When designing multiple level decks with a stairway between them, be sure to take into account the desired tread and rise dimensions, as well as the total run and total rise. This will dictate how far apart the decks can be and how much they can change in elevation.

Building a Stairway

You will begin building your stairway with the most difficult element of it: the stringers. You must decide between the three different types: cleat, built-up, and cutout.

CLEAT. (See Figure 57.) This type of stringer is a solid board. To it are attached small strips of wood, called cleats. Each stair tread will rest on and be supported by these cleats. This is probably the easiest type of stairway to build. It is not as fancy looking as the other two types and will give your deck a more rustic look. Cleat stairways are often used to go from the first floor of a house to the basement.

BUILT-UP. (See Figure 58.) This stringer is made by attaching triangular blocks to a solid board. The treads and risers are fastened to the blocks. Therefore, it is important that all the blocks be attached in the exact location that is needed. This takes a great deal of skill and patience. This type of stringer is not advised because even professional carpenters can find it difficult to build them so they are perfect.

CUTOUT. (See Figure 59.) Cutout stringers are similar in appearance to built-up stringers, but they are made differently. Instead of attaching triangular blocks to the board, triangular sections are cut out of it. If you can cut along a straight line, you will be able to build a stairway using cutout stringers as well as the pros do.

It is important when making cutout stringers to use a board that is wide enough to remain strong after the pieces are cut out of it. Normally, a 2 by 12 is chosen. It should also be free of knots, because they weaken the overall strength of the board. In some instances, it may be necessary to attach a 2 by 6 to the completed stringer to give it additional support (see Figure 60).

Laying Out Stringers

If you will be making cleat or cutout stringers, the layout will be the same and will require the use of a framing square. The first step is to determine the length of the stringer. If you excel in trigonometry, this is not a problem. However, for the rest of us there is a very simple way to determine the length of the stringers. It involves using your framing square and a tape measure.

Let's assume the total rise is 8 feet and the total run is 12 feet. To find the length of the stringer, simply convert those measurements to inches and mark them on a framing square. Thus, on the blade of your framing square you would mark 12 inches and on the tongue you would mark 8 inches. Using the

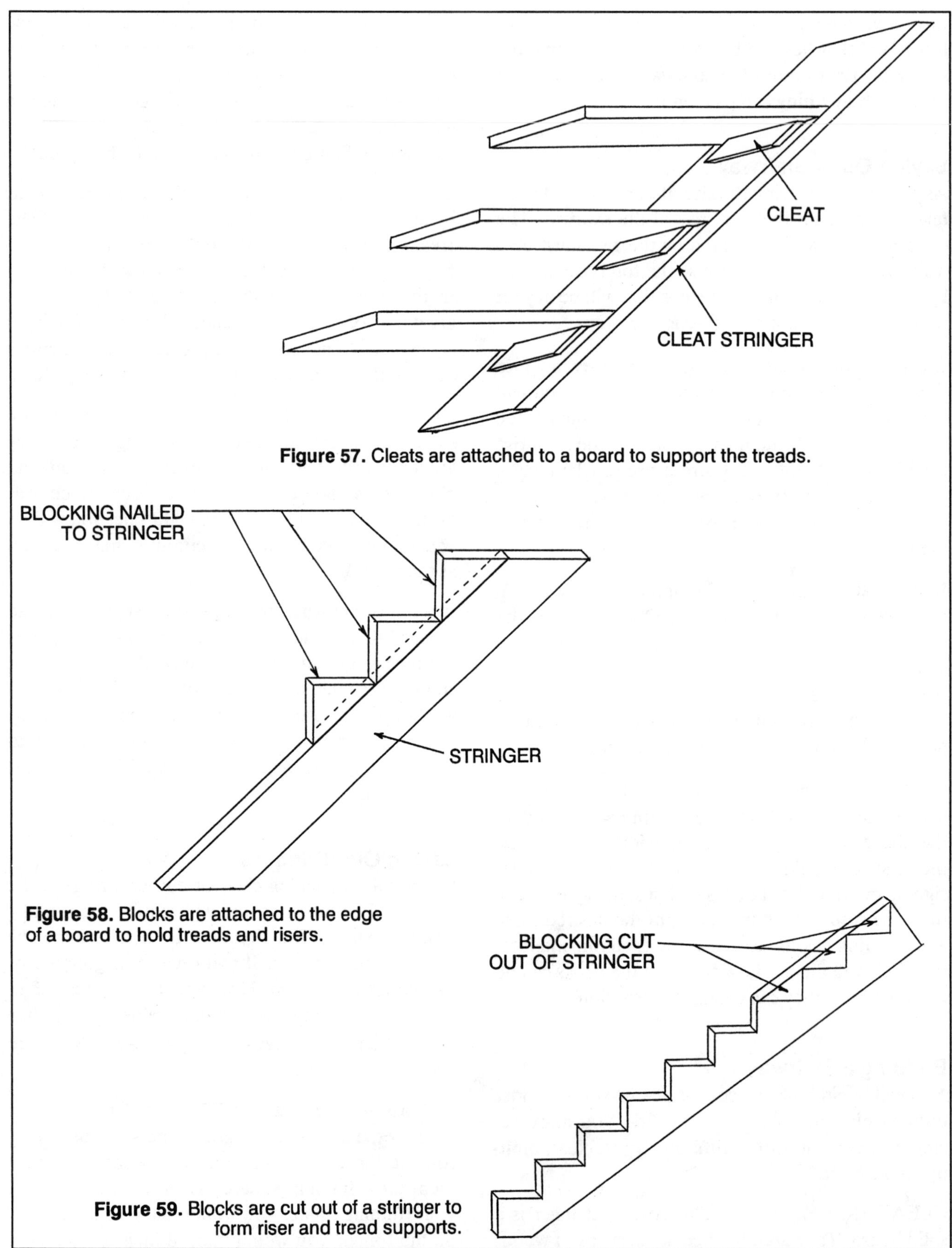

Figure 57. Cleats are attached to a board to support the treads.

Figure 58. Blocks are attached to the edge of a board to hold treads and risers.

Figure 59. Blocks are cut out of a stringer to form riser and tread supports.

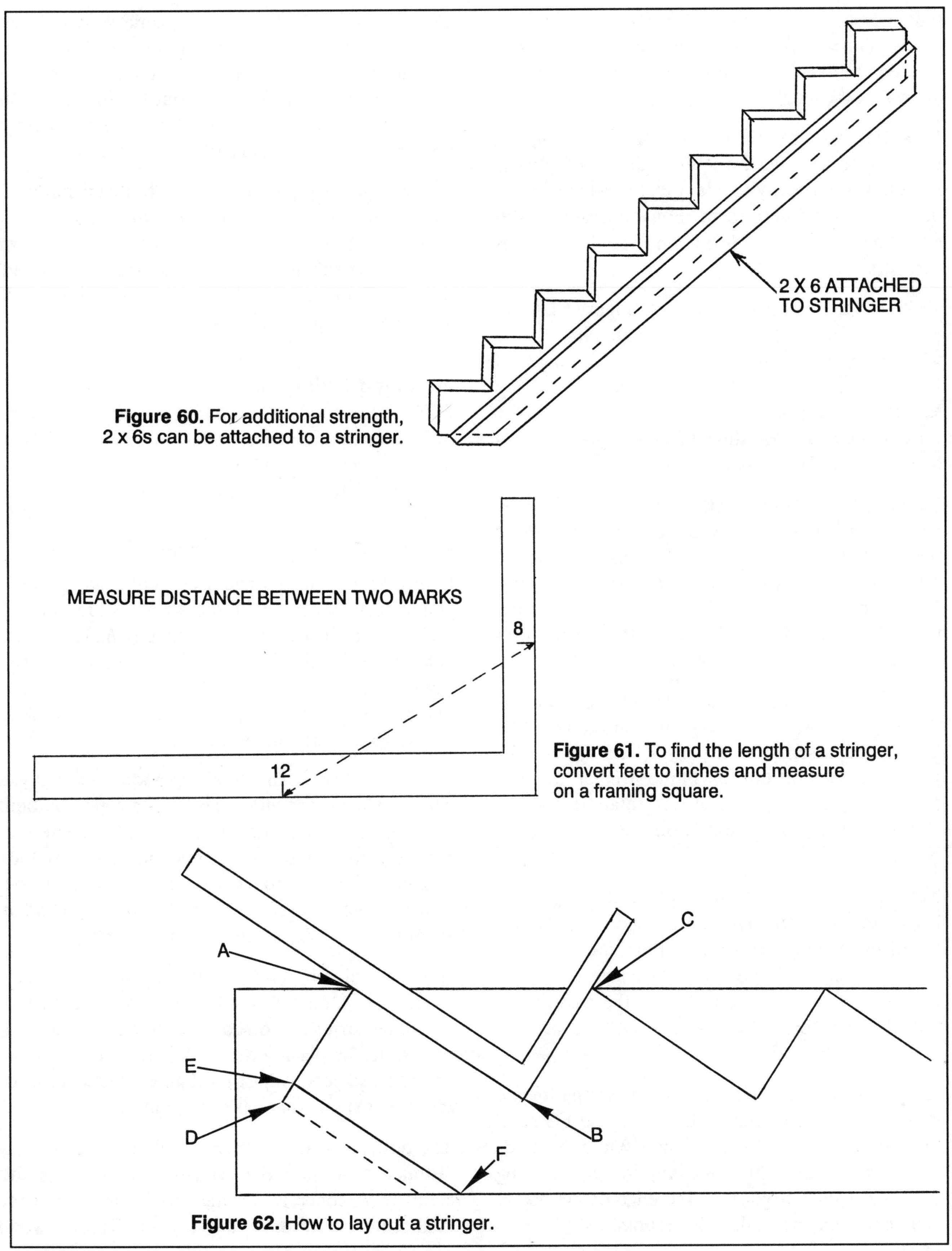

Figure 60. For additional strength, 2 x 6s can be attached to a stringer.

Figure 61. To find the length of a stringer, convert feet to inches and measure on a framing square.

Figure 62. How to lay out a stringer.

tape measure, find the distance between those two points. You would find that it is just about 15 inches (see Figure 61). Converting back to feet, you would know that the length is 15 feet.

However, because the method of connecting the stringers to the deck requires the board to be longer, it is necessary to add 3 feet to whatever you determine this length to be. For our example, this would mean we need 18-foot long boards for use as stringers.

To lay out the first stringer, refer to Figure 62. Mark the tread size on the blade of your framing square, which is point A, and the riser size on the tongue of it, which is point C. Now position the framing square so that points A and C are even with the edge of the board. Holding it firmly in place, draw a line from A to B and from B to C.

Line AB will be your first tread, and line BC will be your second riser. To draw the second tread, move the framing square so that point A matches point C. Again, with the two marks on the framing square flush with the edge of the board, draw the two lines the same as you did the first time. Repeat this process until all the stairs are drawn on the board.

Notice in Figure 62 that the bottom riser and bottom edge that rests on the ground are drawn. The line AD represents the first riser, and the line FG represents the bottom edge of the stringer that rests on the ground. To draw line AD, rotate the square 180° so that points A and B on the blade are reversed.

Now draw a line down the edge of the tongue the length of the riser. This forms line AD. At this point, you will need to subtract the thickness of the tread from line AD. You do this because the rise of the first stair will be correct after the tread is installed, not before. Mark the amount that was subtracted from line AD as point F.

Align your square along line AF so that the tongue is pointing toward point G. Lines AF and FG need to be perpendicular to each other. When the blade is properly aligned along line AF, draw a line along the tongue until it goes off the edge of the board. Where the line meets the edge is point G.

The top is finished off in the same way, only reversed, as shown. Once the first stringer is marked, it is not necessary to mark the second and third in the same manner. Instead, cut out the first one with a circular saw and a hand saw. After it is completely finished, you will be able to use it as a template.

Before doing so, hold it in place to make sure that every element of it is correct and fits properly. If it passes this test, you are ready to use it as a pattern to mark the others. Lay it on the other board and trace the outline of it. This is a much quicker way for laying out the remaining stringers.

Installing Stringers

Different methods of installing stringers are used by different carpenters. Regardless of the method used, the object of installing stringers is to build a stairway that is structurally strong and safe for passage. Figures 63, 64, and 65 show three common methods for attaching the top of the stringer to the deck.

In Figure 63, the stringers are hung using metal connectors. In Figure 64, the stringers are notched out to rest on a ledger strip that is nailed to the header. Notice that they are also nailed or screwed from behind the header. In Figure 65, the stringers run parallel with the joists. They are therefore bolted against the side of the joists.

All three of these methods are good, and you can choose whichever will be easiest for your situation. Temporarily secure the stringers in place. The reason they are not secured immediately is that they may need some minor adjustments. Once they are in place, use a level to check for plumb. Hold it against the riser cut as shown in Figure 66.

If it is not plumb, raise or lower the stringer slightly as needed. After the first has been plumbed, check the other stringers to see that they are level with each other by placing the level across the stringers on the tread cuts. Adjust until all stringers are level with the first one that has been plumbed.

The bottom of the stringers should also be securely fastened to ensure the structural integrity of the stairway. A concrete footing should be poured for anchoring the bottom of the stringers. Treated wood

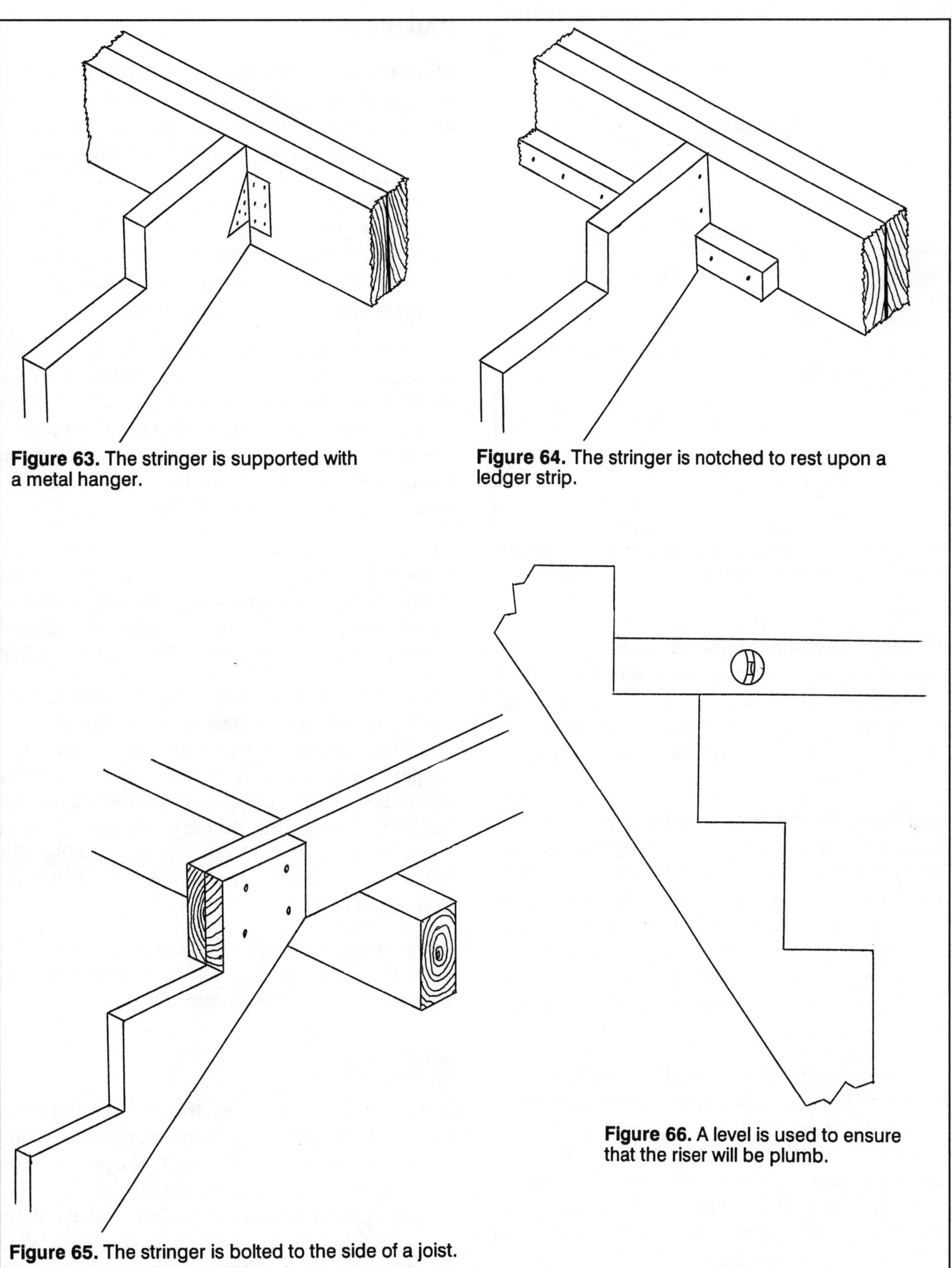

Figure 63. The stringer is supported with a metal hanger.

Figure 64. The stringer is notched to rest upon a ledger strip.

Figure 65. The stringer is bolted to the side of a joist.

Figure 66. A level is used to ensure that the riser will be plumb.

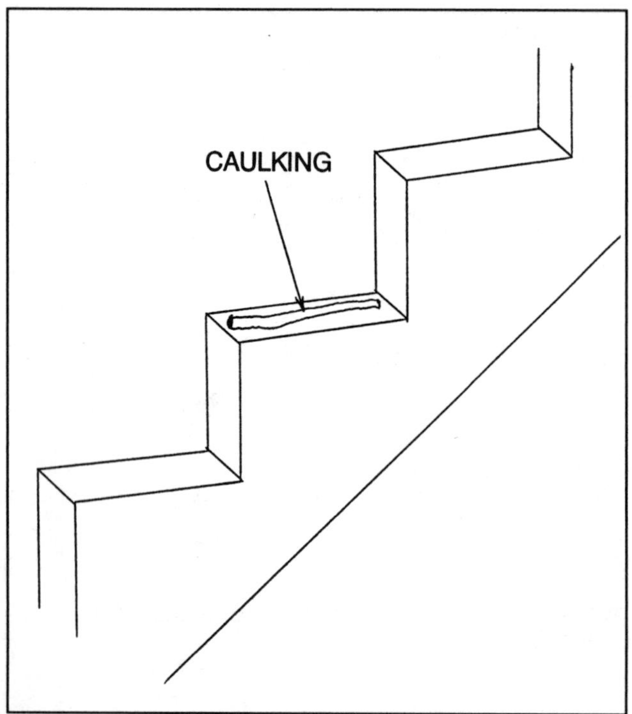

Figure 67. A bead of caulking beneath the treads will prevent them from squeaking.

or metal connectors can be embedded in the concrete to secure the stringers to. It is essential to design this foundation for the stairs so that it goes below the frostline. If not, frost will lift the foundation, and your stairs will end up seriously out of level.

Installing Risers and Treads

After the stringers are in correct position and securely fastened, you are ready to install the risers and treads. The risers should all be installed before you install any of the treads. Because you will not be stepping on the risers, the boards need only be 3/4 inch thick. The treads, however, should be at least 1 1/2 inches thick to support the loads that will be placed on them.

A simple yet effective method for improving the quality of the stairway is to caulk the stringer before nailing the tread to it (see Figure 67). This will eliminate squeaks caused by the friction of the tread rubbing against the stringer when you are using the stairs. Having a silent stairway is very pleasing and gives it a feel of sturdiness and quality when you use it. Squeaks are quite irritating.

RAILINGS

Most stairways and all high-level decks should have railings. Building codes set some minimum guidelines to follow for railing construction. Typically, if a deck is higher than 30 inches off the ground, a railing at least 36 inches high is required. Furthermore, balusters or horizontal members are also required, to prevent children from falling off the deck. Many codes require these to be positioned close enough so that a cylinder of 4 inches in diameter cannot pass between the members.

Generally, railing heights range from 36 to 42 inches, although in some instances when privacy is desired they can be as high as 6 feet. The strongest railing design is one that incorporates posts used in the deck's substructure. Because the posts extend down to the footing where they are securely fastened, they can be moved very little.

There are many railing styles from which to choose. Look through Chapter 9 to see several popular styles. When choosing a railing design, be sure to coordinate it with your house's architectural style. Use the same materials, connections, moldings, and detailing.

If your plans call for railings, it is usually necessary to build and attach the main posts before you nail down the decking. If you do not use the posts that support the deck as part of your railing, it is necessary to bolt posts to the deck's substructure. Do this before you install the decking, and you will have ample room to work. Do it after the decking is installed, and it will require working beneath the deck in cramped quarters.

For greatest strength, bolt the posts using a widely spaced bolt pattern. This will hold each post more securely than a narrow pattern will.

BENCHES

If you want sturdy seating that will last for many years and can serve many purposes, consider adding benches to your deck. The best designs are those that bolt the support posts directly to the deck's substructure. An alternative method is to attach the posts to the decking using angle brackets. When doing so, be sure that the posts are attached directly above a joist. If not, the decking could sag or even break under extreme loads.

The typical bench height is at least 15 inches but not more than 18 inches. If you will be using a bench design that includes a backrest, plan on capping the top of it just as you would a railing. The cap will keep water from soaking down into the supporting boards through exposed end grain. It will also serve as a mini-table to hold food or drinks.

Benches experience a large volume of traffic—your design should reflect that. Make sure that no bolt heads or nuts are protruding in any area around the perimeter of the bench or in any area where they might be rubbed against and cause an injury. Also, use high quality boards for bench construction. The lower grades of lumber are more likely to splinter. It is wise to sand the bench once it is complete to remove any rough spots and to round any corners.

OVERHEADS

Overheads can simply add to the aesthetics of the deck or they can be used to filter light or provide protection from rain. They are typically made out of wood, but if you desire a waterproof roof, there are several materials to choose from, including sheet metal, fiberglass, plastic, slate, glass, and asphalt.

When building overheads, you build in much the same way as you build a deck. If the overhead includes an open design, and its purpose is primarily aesthetic, the design requirements will not be as stringent as for a deck. Usually this type of overhead need only be designed to carry 30 pounds per square foot. Check with the local code enforcement office to verify what the requirements are in your area.

If the overhead will provide protection from rain, it will probably have to be designed according to the same specifications as the deck. The strongest overhead design is that in which the posts supporting the deck continue up and support the overhead as well.

The lowest member of the overhead should be at least the height of a typical doorway, usually 80 inches. Because of their height, it is difficult to build overheads with just a stepladder. It will be much easier and safer and will consume less time if you rent a couple of sections of staging from a local tool rental shop. The few dollars extra expense is money well spent.

POINTS TO REMEMBER

- ☐ Consider adding to the beauty and utility of your deck with advanced deck-building techniques.
- ☐ If stairs are a part of your design, become familiar with the terminology and the different types of stairways. Pay special attention to the riser-to-tread relationship and stair width, as these are prescribed by the building codes.
- ☐ Railings, benches, and overheads can also add to the beauty and utility of your deck design.

7
Deck Accessories and Special Extras

Like the interior of your home, your deck needs proper furnishings and equipment so you can enjoy it to the fullest extent possible. This chapter presents a sampling of amenities for your deck, along with guidelines about the correct uses and benefits of each.

SUNSHADES

If you live in an area of the country that is hot or experiences a lot of sunshine, consider shielding the sun's rays. If your yard lacks the natural protection offered by a large shade tree, consider building an alternative such as a gazebo, trellis, or canopy. If these are more than your budget currently allows, consider purchasing portable sunshades.

Gazebos are quite expensive, but they do serve more than one purpose. With a shingled roof, they will not only shade the sun but provide a dry area sheltered from the rain. If you plan to build it yourself, expect the materials alone for a small gazebo to cost from $700 up. Material costs for large gazebos could range from $2,000 to $4,000.

Trellises and canopies can be built for much less than gazebos. The cost to buy the materials for an average-sized trellis is only a few hundred dollars. If you would like to control the amount of shade on your deck, consider building a trellis with adjustable louvers.

The most familiar portable shade is the old-fashioned canvas umbrella. In the past decade or so, it has experienced a renewed surge of popularity. There are now many companies that make them using modern materials, and you can choose from a multitude of styles. By clustering several of these together you can make a mobile outdoor room.

OUTDOOR FURNITURE

Outdoor furniture has come a long way from the old days when we used to sit on tubular aluminum chairs with scratchy plastic strap seats. Today's outdoor furniture is designed to be durable enough to last for years, practical enough to be used anywhere, and attractive enough to complement almost any setting.

Outdoor furniture is available in a wide range of styles and materials. Shopping for furniture that is perfect for your needs may take some time. As you check out different pieces, consider comfort, durability, weather resistance, and mobility.

Comfort

Comfort is of primary importance. You will not be able to relax on your deck for hours at a time while sitting on furniture that is uncomfortable. You must be certain that any furniture you buy is completely comfortable. When shopping at stores, try out the pieces you are considering. Stretch out in the lounge chairs and find out how they feel. Unless a chair makes you feel like staying in it and taking a long nap, keep shopping.

Durability and Maintenance

Look for furniture that is protected by scratch- and corrosion-resistant finishes. Enamel coatings over steel or wood ensure long life of the furniture and make it easy to maintain. Check the construction of each piece of furniture carefully. Will it withstand constant use? Will it be able to endure the aggressive activities of playful children?

If the upholstery is not made of synthetics that are naturally resistant to decay, be sure that the fabrics have been treated to resist dirt, mildew, and fading. Also, check out the cleaning instructions before you buy any piece of furniture. Cleaning with soap and water is ideal and easy. If special care is needed to clean the furniture, maintaining it will be a little more difficult.

Weather Resistance

Any material available, including stone, is bound to weather to some degree if it spends its entire life outdoors. However, some materials do hold up exceptionally well to the elements. Aluminum, certain types of plastic, and enameled steel fall into this category. Other materials, such as wicker, aren't appropriate for continuous direct exposure to the elements. If you are unsure about a certain piece's ability to withstand the weather, find out before you buy.

Mobility

Heavy iron and wood pieces don't lend themselves well to moving and storing. Ideally, look for furniture that is easily moved to take advantage of sun or shade. Furniture that folds and stacks is quite easy to store. This is especially convenient for those who live in the northern part of the country, where winter snows force them to store furniture in garages or basements during this season.

PEST CONTROLS

There are two ways of controlling uninvited guests —flies, mosquitoes, moths, ants, and others of that sort. One is chemical; the other is non-chemical.

Chemical Insecticides

Chemical insecticides come in either powdered or liquid form and are usually mixed with water before being sprayed. A very common applicator is a tank with a handle on top, which is pumped to build pressure for spraying. Electric foggers are also regularly used to spray insecticides. WARNINGS: Be sure to store any insecticides in a locked compartment that children cannot penetrate. Be certain to follow the manufacturer's instructions carefully and only buy insecticides that are environmentally safe.

Non-Chemical Pest Killers

There are several non-chemical pest killers available that work in different ways. Some models use water to drown the trapped insects. One of the more effective units uses fluorescent "black light" tubes to attract the bugs. A wire cage surrounds the lights in this unit.

On their way toward the light, the insects come in contact with this cage, and the unit zaps them with high-voltage electricity, killing them on contact. The chief drawback to this unit is the noise that occurs when a bug comes in contact with it. However, after a short while most people become immune to the sound of the unit performing its job.

You may find citronella candles or torches useful as a pest repellent. They have a pleasant odor when burned that repels mosquitoes especially well. Citronella candles can be purchased in many hardware stores and mail order catalogs.

HEATERS

Although cold weather discourages insect pests, it can discourage you from using your deck as well. Permanent fireplaces made of brick or stone are quite heavy and must sit on the ground, not on the deck. This means that they are practical only for decks that are relatively low to the ground. They must also be installed during the construction of your deck.

Gas and electric heaters are also available to heat your deck. However, they will only work in enclosed areas such as a greenhouse or an enclosed porch.

Electric heaters are usually silent when operated. Heaters that run on propane or kerosene typically are somewhat noisy when they are being used; however, they are less expensive to operate than electric heaters and normally emit more heat than their electric counterparts. Because of this, they can be used to heat larger spaces than electric heaters are able to heat.

OUTDOOR GRILLS

Whether you're cooking hamburgers or freshly-caught fish, food cooked outside always seems to taste better. Charcoal grills first appeared in America in the early 1950s. It didn't take long for nearly every household to have one. It's no wonder: they are relatively inexpensive, the mess from cooking stays outside, and food cooked on a charcoal fire tastes great.

Even today, outdoor cookers remain one of America's best-selling appliances. There are many from which to choose. Should your unit be built-in, free-standing, on wheels to be rolled around, or portable so that it can easily be taken on camping trips or picnics? And what fuel source will be best for you—electricity, gas, or charcoal? Remember, to get long life from your grill, clean it after each use and keep it protected from the elements.

Charcoal Grills

These range in size from small tabletop hibachis to very large covered wagons. Models made from cast iron last much longer than ones of steel, but are heavier, making them more difficult to move. Cast iron grills aren't as readily available as their steel counterparts. The biggest disadvantages of charcoal grills are the time required to get the briquettes burning and the messy cleanup of the leftover ashes.

Gas Grills

Unlike charcoal grills, gas grills are much easier to start and their heat can be readily fine-tuned. Permanent grills require a natural-gas hookup, and portable ones run on bottled gas.

The secret to getting the unique grilled taste from a gas cooker is to make sure that it uses porous briquettes, such as volcanic rock. As the food cooks, the juices and fats are trapped in the pores and occasionally flare up. It is this action that gives food that great flavor it has when cooked on an outdoor grill.

Electric Grills

Electric grills also use porous briquettes made from ceramic material or volcanic rock. Although they are portable, these units tend not to be as popular as the other two types. One reason is that they are only usable where there is electricity available, reducing their portability. Another reason is that it is harder to regulate their temperature than that of gas grills.

HOT TUBS AND SPAS

Adding a hot tub or spa can turn your deck into a luxurious spot for a relaxing outdoor soak. You'll have to decide where on your deck you will locate it, based on your preference of a sunny or shady location, the amount of privacy, views from the tub or spa, and access to existing electrical service and water.

Keep in mind that a hot tub or spa weighs from 3,000 to 6,000 pounds when filled with water. Because of this extreme weight, a hot tub or spa should be located on a platform that sits on the ground. If you desire to locate a tub or spa on an elevated platform, consult an engineer, as this weight greatly exceeds the heavy load capabilities that an average deck is designed to carry.

As you are planning the location for your hot tub, be sure that you allow enough room for maintenance equipment, heaters, pumps, and filters. These items should be in a location that is easy to get to for servicing. It will also save money in the long run to design the location of your hot tub or spa in such a way that a thick layer of insulation can surround the unit. Well-insulated tub covers are also highly recommended.

An average-sized unit, about 4 feet by 5 feet, will hold 475 gallons of water. The normal temperature for this water when the tub is in use is 100° to 102° F. When you are not using the tub, it is a good idea to turn the thermostat down to 80° or 85°. This saves money, but keeps the tub warm enough so that it will not require too much time to heat up when you want to use it.

However, heating so much water to the temperature required adds considerably to your monthly utility bill. Thick insulation will greatly reduce the rate at which the water cools off, substantially reducing the amount of energy needed to keep the tub at these temperatures. The insulation will save money month after month, and it pays for itself in a short period of time.

Hot tubs and spas are not inexpensive. For a basic model, expect to pay anywhere from $1,700 to $2,500. Hot tubs are usually made from wood, with redwood the material of choice. However, other woods, such as oak, cypress, and teak are occasionally used for hot tub construction.

Spas are almost always made of fiberglass. They offer a much wider range of colors and shapes, with literally hundreds upon hundreds of selections to choose from. When shopping for a spa, make sure that there are no tiny cracks in the fiberglass. While stress cracks are not uncommon, their appearance could indicate that the unit was handled roughly, possibly causing structural weakening.

Most companies that sell hot tubs or spas today sell them in kits that include everything you need for installation and operation. This includes plumbing, heating unit, pump, filter, lint trap, chlorine testing kit, and built-in seats. These kits make it easy for homeowners to assemble the units themselves. However, for safety's sake it's wise to get the assistance of a plumber and an electrician.

SWIMMING POOLS

A swimming pool in your backyard may sound like a luxury item that is outside the capacity of your budget. However, it could be more affordable than you think. Many medium-sized above-ground pools can be purchased for under $1,000.

When you consider the pleasures of early morning dips before work, summertime splashing, and moonlit swims, as well as the exercise benefits, your own pool starts to look like a much better value. By surrounding an above-ground pool with an attractive deck, you can create a delightful resort in your own backyard.

No matter what your budget, it is a good idea to get professional recommendations. Shop around by visiting several locations that specialize in swimming pool sales. If possible, talk to the business owners, or at the very least knowledgeable salespersons, describe your situation, and ask for their advice. Most will cheerfully answer your questions, especially if they want to sell you a pool. However, if you want them to come to your home to do a personal evaluation, expect to pay for this service.

An experienced professional can assure you that the appearance and function of your pool are in line with what your budget will allow and are ideal for your unique situation. Before you hire anyone to perform a professional evaluation of your location, get references and find out if he is a member of the National Spa and Pool Institute. This organization promotes guidelines and standards for pool quality and safety.

PLANTERS

Planters located on your deck can provide brilliant splashes of color that add to the beauty and attractiveness of your overall deck design.

If your planters will be of the smaller, portable type, then it is not necessary to determine a location for them. However, if you would like to incorporate one or more planters into your deck's design as permanent fixtures, you need to choose their locations carefully.

Try to choose a location that will be good for both you and the flowers you intend to plant. Before you design the location of your planter, you'll need to decide the plant varieties you desire. To do so, refer to a good gardening book to see what types of plants grow well in your area. You should also check catalogs and visit a few local nurseries.

LIGHTING

The arrival of sunset need not be a signal that it's time to head indoors. Well-planned outdoor lighting can make your deck as dramatic and inviting at night as it is during the day, and it can allow you to use your deck at any hour you desire.

Too often outdoor lighting consists of nothing more than a single floodlight attached to the exterior of the house. Fortunately, you are not limited to this type of outdoor lighting scheme. There are many possibilities for creating dramatic settings by incorporating a well-designed illumination plan that enhances your deck's appeal.

Lighting to be used for your deck falls into two categories: decorative and functional. Each of these types can be installed permanently or set up temporarily for special occasions. In either case, electricity will most likely be required. Torches, kerosene lanterns, and gas-operated lights are available, but these types are primarily for decorative purposes and are not commonly used.

Developing an ideal plan for your deck may require the assistance of a professional. Advice from landscape architects and electricians is invaluable as you formulate the lighting scheme. Whether you need them for planning purposes or not, it is wise to hire an electrician to do the actual work. Wiring, in general, can be a dangerous task; it is even more so when done outdoors.

FUNCTIONAL LIGHTING

Functional lighting is best described as the light that's necessary to see in order to do any activity. It is neither decorative nor luxurious; rather it is essential. Functional lighting falls into two categories: large area illumination and focused lighting.

Large Area Illumination

As you consider lighting your entire deck area, it is important to remember that it will require much less light than an area of similar size that is indoors. Outdoor light should be lower in intensity than indoor light. This creates an atmosphere that is comfortable and somewhat romantic. It is not desirable to try to make your deck area as bright as the inside rooms of your home.

It is also important to plan the location of the lights so that they don't shine directly in anyone's eyes. It is more efficient and costs less for installation to use fewer bulbs with higher wattage. For example, it is better to plan one fixture with a 300-watt bulb than to plan three fixtures with 100-watt bulbs. You certainly would not want this 300-watt bulb shining directly into anyone's eyes.

There are several ways of accomplishing this goal. One is to mount the lights from 15 to 20 feet overhead, so the light shines onto the deck at about a 45° angle. Another method is to aim the fixtures at walls, ceilings, or other surfaces near the deck and bounce the light off them. Another technique to prevent light from shining directly in someone's eyes is to conceal the lights behind something, such as a valance. Before mounting the light permanently, test these alternatives to see which is right for you.

Focused Lighting

Focused lighting differs from large area illumination in that it is directed at one specific spot. Places that require focused lighting include walkways, stairs, and activity areas such as barbecues, tables for eating or playing games, and other similar spots that require brighter light.

WALKWAYS. Walkways should be well lit to ensure safe passage. Low-level lighting is ideal for this purpose. It is very attractive and is more practical than lights that are positioned higher. Lights mounted high tend to make people have to walk in their own shadows. Nearly all low-level lights require special wire that is capable of being run underground. Professional installation is recommended.

STAIRS. In order of importance, stairs rank at the top of the list of outside areas that need to be well lit. It is especially important that the lights used to illuminate stair areas create no hazards such as casting deceptive shadows. They should be in a location that doesn't cause any glare or create obstacles that would obstruct traffic flow. Excellent locations for these lights are underneath the stair treads or off to the side of the stairway.

ACTIVITY AREAS. Each activity area needs light focused directly on it. Grills, workbenches, card tables, game areas, or any other place a specific activity occurs require additional light. However, each is likely to require light of different intensity. It's best to consider each area individually, providing only enough light to illuminate the particular area. Be sure to put each light on its own switch.

DECORATIVE LIGHTING

While functional lighting is necessary to see, decorative lighting is optional. Its primary purpose is to add beauty and create an atmosphere. This can be done with accent lighting or special occasion lighting.

Accent Lighting

Accent lighting is often used to highlight certain areas that are appealing to look at, such as elements of the landscape or the perimeter of the deck. Accent lighting is used to make a distinctive impression that can be accomplished in no other manner.

PERIMETER LIGHTING. The night-time mood and character of the deck can be greatly enhanced by the installation of miniature lights around its perimeter. Low intensity perimeter lighting is one of the most effective ways to give your deck an elegant appearance in the evening hours. During the daytime, however, you will not want to look at unsightly wires. Be sure these are concealed to eliminate this potential problem.

LANDSCAPE LIGHTING. If you have an element of nature in your yard that is particularly appealing, such as trees, shrubs, or flowers in a planter, illuminating it will augment your deck's night-time appeal.

Special Occasion Lighting

Holidays, special functions, and festivities can be enhanced by the use of special temporary lighting on a deck. Strings of lights could be strung to spell "Happy Birthday" or any other message that might be desired. Whenever temporary lights are used, take extreme care to use them in a safe manner.

Color Lighting

Color lighting requires expert planning. Most colors, especially green, make people look unnatural and sick. Other than focusing the colored light at a waterfall or fountain, it's best not to plan any colored lighting without professional assistance.

LIGHT FIXTURES AND EQUIPMENT

Light fixtures come in thousands of designs, sizes, and prices. However, the bulbs that these use are limited to a few types. Listed from highest intensity to lowest, they are: halogen, mercury vapor, sodium vapor, fluorescent, and regular glass-enclosed filament bulbs.

HALOGEN/QUARTZ. This light has a yellowish tint very similar to a regular incandescent light bulb. However, it extends the light to a wider radius and a much greater distance than a regular light bulb does. This light is best to use when you have a larger area to illuminate, such as an entire backyard.

MERCURY VAPOR. This type of light has a whitish tint to it. It is an economical light when used for extended periods of time. Typically, this type of light is used with a photocell that turns the light on at dark and off at dawn. Mercury vapor light bulbs last approximately 20,000 hours, compared to 1,500 hours for a regular light bulb.

SODIUM VAPOR. This type of light gives off an orange tint. This is the most economical light for use with high wattages and for long periods of time. Until the last five years, this type of light wasn't commonly used for residential purposes; however, it is becoming increasingly popular for home use.

FLUORESCENT. This type of light is not very practical for outdoor situations because it requires special equipment such as high-output ballasts and bulbs, which are very expensive. If your deck has an enclosed patio room, this type of lighting can be used with various colored bulbs to give a different effect. Grow-lights for plants are of the fluorescent type.

FILAMENT/INCANDESCENT. Since Thomas Edison invented this type of light it has done nothing but increase in popularity and uses. This is the easiest type to install, because no special apparatus is required, such as a special encasing for protection. Because this type of lighting is so popular, there are many, many variations of styles from which to choose. However, this is the most expensive type of light to operate. If you will use your lights a great deal, it would be more economical to choose another type. If your light usage is average, this difference in cost should only amount to $5.00 to $10.00 per month.

PLUMBING

Water is a great convenience to have outside your home. Water can be piped to a hose connection, an outdoor sink, or a sprinkler system. In addition, water can be used to create decorative pools that might include a fountain, spray, or waterfall. However, these are closed systems and don't require a continuous flow of water. Only a small amount will need to be added once every week or two to compensate for evaporation.

Installation instructions for any of these items are beyond the scope of this book, and you should consult another source for detailed information. Following are some guidelines for your consideration.

HOSE CONNECTIONS. This simple but essential item is quite inexpensive to install. One may be adequate, but two would be better. Locate them in convenient areas because they will be used often. For northern climates, a special faucet is made that will not freeze. The price is only a few dollars more but is worth the money.

SPRINKLER SYSTEMS. If you are planning to have planters, you will quickly find out that they dry out rapidly. Sprinklers or misting heads can easily be installed to keep the soil moist and eliminate the need for constant watering. Be sure that all materials used are corrosion-proof, such as PVC pipe (plastic).

OUTDOOR SINK. If your deck plan incorporates a grill or barbecue pit, the installation of an outdoor sink will prove to be most useful. Cooking always requires utensils, which in turn require cleaning. Having a sink nearby eliminates the need to make constant trips inside to use one. Cleanup can be completed outdoors, so you won't have to bring the mess inside to wash it.

DECORATIVE POOLS. Decorative pools need not have plumbing to them; rather, they can be filled using a hose. Remember that water weighs more than 8 pounds per gallon. Even in a small pool that is 3 feet square by 2 feet deep, the water alone will weigh approximately 1,100 pounds. If the pool will sit on the deck, consult an engineer for structural safety.

Fountains, sprays, or waterfalls added to the pool offer the sound and sight of moving water, giving the deck added charm and vitality. To accomplish the water movement, electric pumps are used. These range in size from tiny ones with only 1/55 horsepower, up to very large units with many horsepower.

DECORATIVE ITEMS

There are many other items that can be used to enhance your deck and bring delight to you, your children, and the local bird population. Elements such as bird feeders, birdhouses, wind devices, hanging swings, etc., are all good choices. You are only limited by your creative ability. For maximum enjoyment, place these items where they can be viewed from inside your home, as well as from out on the deck.

POINTS TO REMEMBER

- ❑ Outdoor furniture should be chosen for comfort, durability, easy maintenance, weather resistance, and mobility.
- ❑ Chemical insecticides and non-chemical pest killers should be used carefully and safely.
- ❑ Outdoor grills—charcoal, gas, or electric—can add to the usability of your deck.
- ❑ Amenities such as hot tubs and spas, pools, and planters can be incorporated into your deck design.
- ❑ Lighting for your deck may include large area illumination, focused lighting, and decorative lighting.
- ❑ Consider whether you would like to include plumbing for hose connections, an outdoor sink, or a decorative pool as part of your deck design.

8
Protection and Maintenance

Over a period of time all materials deteriorate. There are steps you can take to slow down the deterioration process and to increase the lifespan of your deck by many years. This chapter examines those that are readily available.

The problem of greatest concern for wood decks is decay, which is caused by certain fungi that use the wood for food. Like other plants, these fungi require air, food, moisture, and warmth in order to survive and grow. They grow most rapidly when the temperature is between 70° and 85° F. Lower temperatures, even those well below zero, simply cause the fungi to remain dormant. However, higher temperatures, like those used in a kiln, will kill the fungi.

This does not mean that kiln-dried lumber is no longer susceptible to fungi. Fungi spores are always present in the air, meaning the wood of your deck is always exposed to them. Whenever the conditions are right, these fungi will grow in the wood of your deck.

It is important to protect your deck against decay-causing fungi. The method of protection has two parts: keep the wood dry by not allowing the moisture content to get high enough to support fungal growth; and use fungicides to destroy fungi and prevent their growth. Many of today's preservatives contain not only fungicides but toxins that inhibit the growth of other decay-causing organisms.

The following paragraphs contain information on different products and methods that can be used to protect your deck, keeping it like new for a long time. You will also find information on how to treat different problems that may occur during the life of your deck.

WOOD FILLERS

To protect the wood, preservatives or other finishes are applied to keep the moisture out. Before these are applied, however, cracks, splits, or seams that allow moisture to enter the wood should be filled. Either caulking or putty can be used to do so.

Caulking

In general, caulking falls into one of four categories: synthetic, latex-based, butyl-rubber, and oil-based caulks. Of these, the best are the synthetic caulks. They will far outlast the other caulks, and some of them even come with guarantees of twenty to fifty years. Before you install caulking, be sure the wood is clean and dry. Some of these caulks can be painted; others can't. If you are planning on painting your deck in the future, be sure to use a caulk that can be painted.

Putties

To fill larger holes or cracks in wood, there are several types of putty that can be used successfully. These compounds are pliable and moldable but set up when exposed to air. For use on decks, buy only a putty designed for exterior use. Some of these are advertised as "high performance," but this description is not necessary for the putty to have superior ability to withstand the elements. The best types of putty wood fillers are the fiberglass compounds.

PRESERVATIVES

First and foremost in the battle against decay are preservatives. Wood may be treated with these by the pressure method, in which the wood is impregnated with preservatives under high pressures and temperatures. If the lumber used to build your deck has not been treated with a preservative, it is worthwhile to apply one. Even the decay-resistant species, such as redwood and cedar, benefit from a preservative treatment. Following is a list of different preservatives available.

COPPER NAPHTHENATE. Several of the more popular preservatives of recent years have been recently banned from retail sales because of health risks and danger to the environment. Copper naphthenate, however, is not one of them. It is not toxic to either plants or animals, making it environmentally safe.

Copper naphthenate is dark green and will discolor the wood, leaving it with a green tinge. This green fades slowly, and the wood eventually weathers to its natural color. The use of copper naphthenate is not suggested for redwood because the beautiful red hues turn to a rather unsightly green, eliminating the natural beauty of the wood. There are other products that are much more appropriate for use on redwood.

Wood treated with copper naphthenate can be painted, but it may take two coats of paint to hide the green tinge completely. For maximum deck lifespan, treat the wood with it every third year.

CREOSOTE. Creosote is one preservative that has been banned in recent years from retail sales, although wood treated with creosote may still be available. This is the preservative most railroad companies use to protect the wooden railroad ties that the steel track sits on. It is made from coal tar and is mildly toxic to plants and animals.

Creosote is black, and wood that has been treated with it is a very dark brown or black. In many areas of the country used railroad ties are sold at building supply stores. Even though these ties are no longer strong enough to support trains, they still have a useful life remaining. If you purchase wood that has been treated with creosote, remember that it cannot be painted.

CHROMATED COPPER ARSENATE (C.C.A.). This product is an arsenic compound. As such, it is very effective at stopping plant growth but is also toxic to animals. It, too, has been banned from retail sales in recent years because of the danger it poses to plants, animals, and people.

C.C.A. is still widely used in the pressure treatment process. It is so effective that it is used for protecting wood that will be submerged in water. Wood that has been treated with this compound for below-ground or in-the-water uses is labeled ".80 C.C.A."

For above-ground uses, wood so treated is labeled ".40 C.C.A." It does discolor the wood, turning it a light to medium green. If you want to paint the wood, it is necessary to let the treated wood weather first. This weathering period is from three months to a year, depending on the manufacturer's guidelines.

Application Methods

There are two methods for applying preservatives. For both, rubber gloves and other protective clothing should be worn. Only perform this routine in a well-ventilated area, preferably outdoors. Be sure to follow the manufacturer's directions carefully.

BRUSHING AFTER DECK IS COMPLETED. This method is the least desirable of the two because it is nearly impossible to cover the wood completely once all the pieces have been attached together. Initially, if possible, try to use the next method to treat your deck with preservatives. For subsequent treatments every third year, however, brushing the preservative on the deck is the only method available.

DIPPING EACH PIECE SEPARATELY. This is

the preferred method. To use this method you need not have a special dipping trough. A simple, temporary one is easy to make. You will need a large plastic sheet without any holes. These can be purchased at any hardware store for a few dollars.

To make the trough, lay several boards in two parallel stacks about 8 inches high and approximately 1 foot apart. Stack boards on each end to form a rectangular box. Now lay the plastic sheet over this form, being careful not to puncture the sheet. Stack weight on the plastic to hold it in place. Pour the preservative into the plastic, and the dipping trough is ready for use. The lumber need not stay in the trough for a soak. Simply dipping it to cover the entire surface is sufficient.

After dipping, you need to let the lumber dry before using it. Plan on a few days in the sunshine to accomplish this. The boards should be placed so there is plenty of circulation around them, preferably standing on end and leaning against something. Try to avoid stacking them, as the ones in the middle of the pile will remain wet.

Although this method is quite effective, it isn't as good as the pressure treatment process, because the preservative doesn't completely penetrate each board. When using boards that have been dipped, it is necessary to coat each end thoroughly with a heavy coat of preservative whenever a board is cut.

WOOD FINISHES

All species of wood are susceptible to damage due to the elements. Even redwood, which has a very high resistance to natural deterioration, quickly changes color and becomes stained when exposed to constant water. To prolong that new look, to change the color of a deck to make it fit an architectural style, or to protect against staining, apply a paint, stain, sealer, or repellent. Any deck will benefit from one of these wood finishes.

Sealers and Repellents

Resin-based sealers such as varnishes and polyurethanes are not recommended for exterior use on decks. They do not form a watertight film on the wood. It is also possible for them to begin to wear and peel in a period as short as six months. The only exception to this is the fiberglass and resin coating that was discussed in Chapter 3.

There are several water repellents available today. Also known as water sealers, these clear liquids protect the wood and prolong its natural beauty. They typically don't change the color of the wood, although they do tend to darken it slightly. Some of these products are designed especially for redwood. They are intended to preserve the original reddish hues and prevent the redwood from turning gray as it weathers. If you like the natural look of wood, a clear water repellent should be used.

Stains

The appearance that stains provide falls between a natural finish and a painted finish. Stains come in two shade ranges: transparent and solid. Transparent and semi-transparent stains allow the wood grain to remain visible. Solid color stains look very similar to paint; they don't allow the natural grain of the wood to show through.

Stains are available in both water- and oil-based types. Generally speaking, the oil-based types are more suited for deck application because they are more durable. However, there have been many improvements made in the water-based stains in recent years, and the quality of some rivals those of the oil-based variety. Water-based stains are much easier to work with because cleanup requires only water. A major stain manufacturer has recently introduced an oil-based stain that requires only water for cleanup. This product works quite well.

When choosing a stain for your deck, be sure that it is wear resistant. For best penetration and maximum durability, allow the deck to weather for one or two months before the stain is applied. Brushing or rolling is the usual method of application, but spraying can also be used if provisions are made for over-spray and if the equipment is suitable for use with stains.

Paints

Paint is typically used on older decks, or newer

decks that are built with less expensive wood. Because paint is not translucent, it is often used to cover defects that are common in lower grades of lumber. Paint is also available in a wide range of colors, giving you more possibilities for the appearance of your deck.

The negative aspects of using paint include the additional labor required to apply the paint and the added maintenance involved with painted decks. With the exception of marine grades, paint is not as durable as the other types of finishes. Decks that are painted are likely to need an additional coat every year or two. Marine grade paints last much longer but they are very expensive, costing as much as $100 per gallon.

Paints, like stains, are available in water- and oil-based types. The oil-based paints of today do not contain the linseed oil or lead that oil-based paints of a few years ago contained. They are much safer for the environment, and their aroma is not nearly as overpowering as it used to be. Most oil-based paints today are alkyds.

When purchasing a paint for your deck, make sure that it is designed for that use. Most paints are not designed to withstand the abuse of being continually walked upon. The paint that you choose will probably have a gloss finish, as flat and semi-gloss finishes will get scuffed and dirty much more easily than the gloss finish will.

It is advisable to use an oil-based primer before painting your deck. This is especially true in the case of redwood or western red cedar. Water-based primers may dissolve and absorb some of the water-soluble substances in these woods and discolor the paint.

For more convenience and a superior job, prime and paint the deck's structure before the decking is installed. This allows you easy access to all the members of the deck and permits nearly complete coverage of each piece. The decking should be covered with one coat of primer and two coats of paint.

When painting, be sure the wood is clean, dry, and free of grease or oil. Any grease or oil residue could prevent the paint from bonding to the wood and the result would be peeling paint in a very short period of time. For maximum bonding strength, paint at a time when the paint will be able to dry slowly, such as in the evening. Hot weather will cause the paint to dry too rapidly, weakening its bonding ability.

PREVENTIVE MAINTENANCE

For maximum deck lifespan, you can perform preventive maintenance that will eliminate potential problems before they occur. Consider the abuse that a deck experiences: rain makes it swell and shrink, causing twisting and warping of the boards; the sun's ultraviolet rays break down the wood's tissue, causing it to discolor; constant traffic wears down the surface and grinds in dirt; and leaves and other scraps get caught between boards, trapping moisture and causing mildew and decay.

There are several areas on decks that are more likely to experience problems in a relatively short period of time. Knowing those areas, and taking precautions to avoid the problems before they occur, will enhance your deck's durability.

Stairs

Stairs probably experience the heaviest traffic of the entire deck. As a result, they are likely to show signs of wear before any other area of the deck. This is especially true of stairs that lead to the yard. Particles of dirt and sand get tracked from the yard onto the stairs, where they are deposited. The constant use grinds this dirt into the wood of the stairs and rapidly wears off the finish. Once the finish is worn off, the grinding dirt particles underfoot begin to wear down the wood itself, just as sandpaper would.

Some preventive steps are easily taken. One simple but important step is to sweep the stairs regularly. By removing dirt and sand, you will remove most of the abrasives that cause damage. Another preventive measure is to coat the stairs regularly with the wood finish you have chosen. By coating two or three times a season, the dirt particles will never be able to get to the actual wood and cause damage.

A third preventive step involves the installation of a waterproof, non-skid covering on the stair treads.

These can be purchased at most hardware stores. They will not only protect the deck from abrasive dirt but will improve safety when the stairs are wet.

Water Runoff

Areas that experience water runoff from a roof are likely to discolor much sooner than the rest of the deck. They are also much more susceptible to mildew and decay. The installation of a gutter and downspout system is highly recommended to prevent water from landing on the deck.

Shaded Locations

Areas that are hidden from the sun take longer to dry than those that experience the drying power of sunshine. Places like the area beneath a movable planter and the location beneath benches and chairs are likely to stay moist for longer periods of time. This allows mildew and eventually fungi to develop. To prevent this from occurring, regularly change the location of the movable objects on your deck, allowing all areas a chance to dry out completely.

Regular Upkeep

Cleaning your deck regularly will not only keep it looking beautiful, it will extend its lifespan. Dirt attracts moisture and causes undue wear on a deck. An occasional blast from a garden hose will wash the dirt away. When cleaning, remove leaves, dirt, and other items that have gathered between boards. These prevent air circulation, which carries away moisture, keeping your deck healthy.

The maintenance suggested may seem like more trouble than it's worth. It really isn't. It is not necessary to get on your hands and knees to scrub the deck. These maintenance tips do not require painstaking hours of labor. A few minutes spent now and then to sweep off and hose down the deck are insignificant compared to the benefits received from doing so.

DEALING WITH PROBLEMS

From time to time, problems may occur. However, they are usually the result of inadequate or lack of protective wood finish, lower quality materials, or lack of regular maintenance. If your deck is suffering from mildew, decay, nail stains and water stains, uneven color from weathering, or termite damage, the following paragraphs will explain how to correct these problems.

Mildew and Decay

If your deck has developed areas of mildew, it is important to correct the problem immediately before it leads to the more serious problem of decay. Caused by the growth of certain fungi, mildew can easily be removed. However, by dealing with the mildew, you are only treating the symptom, not the problem.

The root of the problem is too much moisture in the location where the mildew developed. Once the mildew is removed, steps must be taken to correct the moisture problem. Determine the reason for the excess moisture, which might be caused by excess water runoff, lack of ventilation, trapped leaves and dirt, or lack of sunshine. Take measures to correct the situation.

To remove mildew, clean the area with a stiff brush and a household cleaner. Many bathroom cleaners contain mildewcides that kill the mildew, making them an ideal choice for your deck. Be cautious of cleaners that contain bleach, as this will cause discoloration of the wood.

For larger, more difficult areas of mildew, it may be necessary to use a heavy-duty cleaner designed for the task. Trisodium phosphate (TSP) is a common and effective cleaner, although it is an acidic compound and is hazardous to skin, eyes, and the environment. Other commercial cleaners are available, with different active ingredients. Whichever you choose, be careful to follow exactly the manufacturer's instructions for use.

Nail Stains

Unless stainless steel or aluminum nails were used in the deck's construction, nail stains will occur. Redwood and cedar are both prone to nail stains. Typically, nail stains penetrate deeply into the wood, and for this reason are difficult to remove.

Oxalic acid, which is white and crystalline, is almost a wonder substance when used to restore natural wood color. It was first discovered in the juice of a species of wood sorrel, and it can be used to remove nail stains, water stains, and restore weathered wood almost back to its original color.

If oxalic acid is used to remove nail stains, they will reappear in a relatively short period of time, unless preventive steps are taken. Before using the oxalic acid, use a nailset to sink the nails below the wood's surface. Fill the consequent holes with a high quality wood filler and wait the required time for it to harden. This will prevent the nail stains from recurring.

Oxalic acid is sold in many building supply stores. To use it, simply mix with water according to the manufacturer's directions. Other products for cleaning and restoring color to your deck are available that include oxalic acid as an active ingredient. These may not require mixing with water, but are premixed and intended for use straight from the can.

Water Stains

Areas of the deck that are persistently soaked with water, such as runoff from the roof or splashing onto the deck from a spa, will develop water stains. If possible, eliminate the source of the water. If that isn't an option, it is necessary to treat the areas with water repellent every six months.

If water stains have already developed, there are several methods of improving their appearance. One way is to coat the deck with a sealer and paint it, which will hide the water stains. Another alternative is to treat the deck with oxalic acid to restore it to its original color. After this is completed, it will be necessary to coat the deck with water repellent to prolong the new look.

You may prefer the weathered look over that of a new deck. If so, the third alternative is to speed up the weathering process on the entire deck. This is accomplished by using household bleach or a mixture of baking soda and detergent.

For decks of redwood or cedar, use the household bleach. Brush it evenly on the dry deck surface. Be sure there are no overlap marks or spots of thicker coverage. Once the surface is covered, spray a light coating of water with your garden hose every half hour, waiting one hour before applying the first coat of water.

For decks made of other woods, use a mixture of 2 pounds of baking soda, a short squirt of dish detergent, and a gallon of water. Apply the mixture with a mop, in the same manner as you would the bleach, being careful to spread it evenly. Wait approximately two to three hours, rinse, and apply a second coat.

Uneven Color from Weathering

As your deck weathers, it may not fade evenly. Areas that receive more sunshine are likely to fade faster than areas that experience more shade. Dealing with this problem is similar to dealing with water stains. Use the same alternatives that are used to solve water stain problems (see section above).

Termites

Termites are a problem in the lower two-thirds of the United States. They fall into two classes: dry-wood and subterranean. Their main food is wood, and your deck could be their next meal. Preventive steps should be taken to ensure that your deck doesn't become their target.

Dry-wood termites are the less harmful of the two varieties, although they are more difficult to control. They fly to the wood instead of coming up from the ground as subterranean termites do. Dry-wood termites are primarily found within 200 miles of the coast in southern states from California to South Carolina.

They bore into the wood and hollow out chambers inside it. The chambers are connected by tunnels. Needless to say, these chambers and tunnels weaken the timbers to the point that they are not usable. Dry-wood termites are seldom seen, remaining the entire time inside the wood.

Subterranean termites are found as far north as Maine and Washington state. They thrive in warm, moist soil where there is an abundance of wood. As they survive and prosper, they are continually looking for more food. They build tunnels about 1/4 to 1/2 inch wide to their next source of food, where they will bore into it and hollow out the interior in honeycomb fashion. Preventive steps are easily taken.

The first step in guarding against these termites is to design your deck so that no wood member comes in contact with the ground. Foundation piers should be at least 12 inches above ground level to prevent the termites from climbing up into the wood of your deck.

Another step that should be taken during the construction phase is to remove all scrap lumber from the job site daily. If you leave it lying around on the ground, it is likely to attract termites. It's much better to clean up daily.

A third step is to use a wood preservative. These contain ingredients that prevent termites from attacking your deck. The fourth and best method of preventing termite infestation is to use a special treatment on the soil around your foundation.

One such solution that has been effectively used in the past is a combination of water, chlordane, aldrin, dieldrin, and heptachlor. This solution is sold premixed at hardware and home improvement stores. This shouldn't be necessary for the majority of decks. Only use this method if termites are severe in your area and there is evidence that the preservative used on your deck is not sufficient protection.

If all these methods have been tried, but the termite problem continues, you should seek the assistance of a professional exterminator.

POINTS TO REMEMBER

- ❑ Wood fillers, such as caulking and putties, should be applied to clean, dry wood.
- ❑ Wood preservatives are the homeowner's primary armor against wood decay.
- ❑ Wood finishes, such as sealers and repellents, stains, and paints, can protect wood from decay and weathering.
- ❑ Preventive maintenance is the best protection for stairs and shaded locations. Also look for water runoff and plan on regular upkeep for your deck.
- ❑ Mildew and decay, nail stains, water stains, uneven color, and termites are all treatable problems if caught early.

9
A Collection of Deck Ideas

The decks shown on the following pages were built by professionals. They are included in the book to help you get ideas for your own deck. While your exact needs will most likely be different from the needs of the owners of these decks—each family's desires are unique—you will still benefit from these photos. There are many ideas illustrated. Pick and choose among the different shapes, styles, rail designs, decking patterns, and bench placements. By choosing what you like best, you will come up with your own unique design that you can enjoy for years to come. *All photos in this chapter courtesy of Archadeck.*

An elevated deck gives a great view and doesn't use up any of the back yard's space.

Homeowners can sun themselves on the lower level or relax in a bubbly spa on the upper level.

An attractive deck design can turn your back yard into a mini-resort.

Part of the deck includes a screened porch, giving the homeowner a deck with greater versatility.

Multiple layers turn what would have been an ordinary deck into something special.

A raised deck meets the top edge of an above-ground pool.

An attractive deck design and appealing landscaping beautify this home's back yard.

The lattice work and overhead give this deck setting just the right appeal.

Shaded by the tree in the center and surrounded by the flowers in planters, this deck offers an inviting location for informal conversation.

A covered spa allows for warm soaking anytime.

This unique design would make any back yard more inviting.

This two-level deck breaks up the expanse yet provides plenty of space for large pool parties.

This free-standing deck with overhead provides a perfect wooded retreat.

A deck provides enjoyment for all ages—from toddler to retiree.

The brick perimeter around the edge of this pool meets the deck perfectly for an attractive flush-mounted appearance.

A spacious low-level deck with surrounding benches is ideal for a range of outdoor activities.

This handsome deck design turns the back yard into an appealing location for relaxation.

The railings give this deck a classic look and keep kids safely enclosed.

A free-standing enclosed deck makes a great outdoor activity center.

Decks can be designed for almost any location, providing a flat surface even on steep slopes.

The intricate deck surrounding the in-ground pool brings the beach to the back yard.

A well-planned deck will provide years of enjoyment.

Various angles in design are used to create an inviting deck.

This overhead diffuses direct rays of the sun as well as providing a cozy atmosphere.

A waterproof overhead allows the homeowner to use the deck in rain or shine.

The design of this deck enhances the great view.

Front yard or back, a deck can be a great part of any home.

An overhead can add a atmosphere of seclusion to virtually any deck.

People and pets alike can experience the benefits of a well-planned deck.

The addition of a spa puts the finishing touch on this handsome deck.

This multi-level deck features a lower level set amongst the trees to provide plenty of shade and an upper level that provides plenty of sun.

Appendices

1. CHECKLISTS

The following checklists have been compiled with the intention of helping you complete a thorough analysis of your deck needs and to guide you as you proceed with your deck project. It's impossible for them to contain all the information and questions necessary for a complete analysis of every person's unique circumstances. Nevertheless, once they have been filled out, they will constitute a very detailed summary of the information you need to formulate your deck plan. Photocopy these checklists and use them throughout the entire deck project from start to finish. You will find them a very valuable resource.

Checklist #1
DECK BUILDER'S MASTER CHECKLIST

1. Determine deck's functions (use Checklist #2). ❑
2. Check building and zoning codes. ❑
3. Decide whether building or zoning codes need to be appealed (use Checklist #3 for appeals).
4. Check deed for restrictive covenants and easements. ❑
5. Determine the existing microclimates (use Checklist #4). ❑
6. Study the existing ground conditions (use Checklist #5). ❑
7. Determine possible deck locations (use Checklist #6). ❑
8. Determine deck style that will be aesthetically pleasing (use Checklist #7). ❑
9. Draw plan view sketch of property (use Checklist #8). ❑
10. Draw preliminary sketches of deck design on copies of plan view sketch. ❑
11. Evaluate sketches using Checklists #2, #4, #5, #6, & #7. ❑
12. Consult with architect or building designer (optional). ❑
13. Draw final sketch of deck design. ❑
14. Estimate cost of materials and construction (use Checklist #9). ❑
15. Draw (or hire drafter to draw) working plans to scale (use Checklist #10). ❑
16. Prepare detailed materials list (use Checklist #9). ❑
17. Obtain building permits. ❑
18. Shop for best deal on materials. ❑
19. Choose at least three contractors from whom to get estimates (optional—use Checklist #11). ❑
20. Decide which contractor to hire (optional—use Checklist #11). ❑
21. Prepare contract (optional—use Checklist #12). ❑
22. Arrange financing and insurance if necessary. ❑
23. Buy materials and begin construction (use Chapters 5 & 6). ❑
24. Schedule appointments for building inspector to examine work at necessary stages of construction. ❑

Checklist #2
DETERMINING DECK'S FUNCTIONS

1. Check all activities that apply:

   Family cookouts ❑
   Sunbathing ❑
   Leisurely rest and relaxation ❑
   Dancing ❑
   Reading ❑
   Socializing ❑
   Large get-togethers ❑
   Swimming ❑

2. Would you like a built-in barbecue pit? ❑
3. Would you like a specially designed place for your gas or charcoal grill? ❑
4. Would you like a built-in hot tub? ❑
5. Will you want to build your deck around a swimming pool? ❑
6. Do you desire a weathertight storage area somewhere on your deck? ❑
7. Do you desire a fence-type railing surrounding the deck to form an enclosed play area for young children? ❑
8. Would you like a screened section of deck to protect you from flying insects? ❑
9. Will you be purchasing portable deck furniture, or do you desire built-in seating and tables? ❑
10. How many people will be using the deck at any one time? Estimate number of:

    Family ❑
    Friends ❑
    Neighbors ❑
    Relatives ❑

11. Determine total number of people your deck will need to accommodate. ❑
12. Keep this information for reference during planning process. ❑

Checklist #3
APPEALING ZONING OR BUILDING CODES

1. Get necessary forms at Code Enforcement Office. ❑
2. Review forms several times to become familiar with them. ❑
3. Talk to Code Enforcement Officer about your appeal. ❑
4. Attend next public hearing as a spectator. ❑
5. After meeting, talk to several people who appealed to get their advice. ❑
6. Develop solid reasons why your appeal should be granted:

   A. The financial hardship that will occur if appeal is not granted. ❑
   B. Reasons the code should not apply to you in this instance. ❑
   C. Unique circumstances that require you to apply for an exception to the code. ❑

7. Fill out application forms and turn in to Code Enforcement Office. ❑
8. Talk to neighbors to get their comments about your appeal. ❑
9. With friendly discussion, try to win neighbors to your point of view. ❑
10. Develop solid responses to any remaining negative comments. ❑
11. Ask several people who support your appeal to testify at the upcoming public hearing. ❑
12. Go to public hearing and present your case to the board in a professional and courteous manner. ❑
13. If required, record the favorable decision at the Registry of Deeds. ❑

Checklist #4
DETERMINING MICROCLIMATES

1. Determine which direction each side of your house faces. ❑
2. Draw sketch of property indicating North, South, East, and West. ❑
3. Install an inexpensive outdoor thermometer on each side of the house. ❑
4. In a journal, record all four temperatures every two hours, for seven consecutive days. ❑
5. At the same time that temperatures are recorded, check and record wind direction. ❑
6. At the same time that temperatures and wind direction are recorded, check the amount of sunshine and record in journal. ❑
7. Keep all information for reference during planning process. ❑

Checklist #5
EVALUATING SITE CONDITIONS

1. Draw rough sketch of property. ❑
2. Record on sketch all pertinent landmarks (low areas, high areas, large boulders, steep slopes, etc.). ❑
3. Dig several holes in prospective deck areas. ❑
4. Record locations of holes on sketch. ❑
5. Record soil types found in each hole (sand, clay, bedrock, etc.). ❑
6. If difficult ground conditions are found, such as a high water table or the presence of clay, consult a soil scientist. ❑
7. Hire soil scientist to perform initial evaluation (use Checklist #11). ❑
8. Ask soil scientist if special foundation designs will need to be incorporated in deck design. ❑
9. Ask soil scientist for any additional foundation recommendations. ❑
10. Keep all information for reference during planning process. ❑

Checklist #6
CHOOSING A DECK LOCATION

1. Complete Checklists #2, #4, and #5. ❑
2. Using information contained in those checklists, evaluate all possible deck locations. ❑
3. Eliminate all less desirable locations, and keep two best possibilities. ❑
4. Rate each one on scale of one to ten according to the following:

	Choice A	Choice B
Cost to build	_______	_______
Privacy	_______	_______
Proximity to play areas	_______	_______
Proximity to kitchen	_______	_______
Proximity to bathroom	_______	_______
Amount of sunshine	_______	_______
Amount of wind	_______	_______
Convenience for installing plumbing	_______	_______
Convenience for installing electrical	_______	_______
Feasibility of modifying or changing deck in the future	_______	_______
Ease of construction	_______	_______
Special features	_______	_______
Capacity for accommodating all desired functions	_______	_______
Effect on traffic patterns	_______	_______

5. Total the score for each possible location. _______ _______
6. Unless scores are quite close, choose the location that earned the highest score. _______

Checklist #7
CHOOSING A DECK STYLE

1. Complete Checklists #2, #4, #5, #6, and #8. ❑
2. Read section in Chapter 1 on aesthetics and style. ❑
3. View different styles in Chapter 9 to get ideas. ❑
4. Determine house style. ❑
5. Decide which deck will best complement your house style: low-level, high-level, multi-level, or roof. ❑
6. Over several days, draw different designs on sketches completed in Checklist #8. ❑
7. Using Checklists #2, #4, #5, and #6, evaluate each sketch for good and bad points. ❑
8. Prepare a final sketch incorporating good ideas and eliminating drawbacks. ❑
9. Go through checklists again with this design. ❑
10. Make minor revisions until design and style are exactly what is desired. ❑

Checklist #8
DRAWING SKETCH OF PROPERTY

1. Determine size and shape of property. ❑
2. On large sheet of paper, draw property boundaries. ❑
3. Draw outline of house. ❑
4. Using a dotted line, draw zoning setback restrictions. ❑
5. Illustrate on sketch North, South, East, and West. ❑
6. Illustrate on sketch these features:

   Driveway ❑
   All walkways ❑
   Steep slopes ❑
   Mature trees ❑
   Landscape features (pond, flower bed, etc.) ❑
   Any easements that affect property ❑
   Underground utilities ❑
   Any other important features ❑

7. Make approximately 25 photocopies of completed sketch. ❑

Checklist #9
PREPARING MATERIALS LIST

1. Read Chapter 3 and Chapter 4. ❑
2. Complete Checklist #10. ❑
3. Make photocopies of worksheets in Chapter 4. ❑
4. Using the working plans, record on worksheets the materials needed for:

    - Footings ❑
    - Foundation piers ❑
    - Posts ❑
    - Beams ❑
    - Joists ❑
    - Bridging ❑
    - Bracing ❑
    - Decking ❑
    - Stringers ❑
    - Treads ❑
    - Risers ❑
    - Newel posts ❑
    - Balusters ❑
    - Horizontal railing ❑

5. Determine quantities and sizes of nails needed. ❑
6. Determine what is needed for metal connectors. ❑
7. Determine quantity of preservative, stain, or paint needed. ❑
8. Consolidate information on worksheets into one material list. ❑
9. Save worksheet for reference during building process. ❑

Checklist #10
DRAWING WORKING PLANS

1. Complete Checklists #2, #4, #5, #6, #7, and #8. ❑
2. Read Chapter 2. ❑
3. Acquire necessary tools listed in Chapter 2:

   Drawing board ❑
   T-square ❑
   Triangles ❑
   Architect's scale ❑
   Quality drawing paper ❑
   Pencils ❑

4. Determine which scale to use. ❑
5. Referring to tables in Chapter 2 and deck sketch from Checklist #8, draw (in pencil) the following plans:

   Plan view ❑
   Foundation plan ❑
   Joist & beam framing ❑
   Elevation drawing ❑
   Cross-section ❑
   Electrical plan (optional) ❑
   Plumbing plan (optional) ❑

6. Check all dimensions, carefully comparing drawings to ensure no mistakes have been made. ❑
7. Have architect or engineer review plans (optional). ❑

Checklist #11
CHOOSING A CONTRACTOR

1. Get recommendations from friends and neighbors. ❑
2. Get recommendations from material suppliers (lumberyards, plumbing wholesalers, etc.). ❑
3. Make initial appointments with several contractors. ❑
4. Get names and addresses of past customers from each contractor. ❑
5. Get bank and credit references from each contractor. ❑
6. Interview past customers. ❑
7. Examine contractors' work. ❑
8. Ask homeowners if contractor was:

   Punctual ❑
   Cooperative ❑
   Reliable ❑
   Knowledgeable ❑
   Pleasant to work with ❑
   Professional ❑
   Helpful ❑

9. Ask what homeowner did not like about contractor. ❑
10. Choose three contractors from whom to get cost estimates. ❑
11. Upon receiving estimates, ask each to give time frame to start and finish job. ❑
12. Decide which contractor to hire. ❑
13. Check bank and credit references. ❑
14. Get copies of contractor's insurance documents. ❑
15. Prepare contract (use Checklist #12). ❑

Checklist #12
PREPARING A CONTRACT

1. Choose a contractor (use Checklist #11). ❑
2. Refer to sample contract in Appendix 2. ❑
3. Using sample contract as example, prepare contract including:

   Set of working blueprints ❑
   Detailed descriptions of all materials to be used ❑
   Detailed descriptive list of all work and duties to be performed ❑
   Time schedule for work to be completed ❑
   Method of payment ❑
   Provision for lien waiver ❑
   Penalties for failure to complete within specified time period ❑
   Detailed written guarantees ❑

4. Schedule appointment to review contract with contractor. ❑
5. Make any revisions resulting from meeting. ❑
6. Bring contract to lawyer for review (optional). ❑
7. Sign contract. ❑

2. SAMPLE CONTRACT

CONTRACT

1. PARTIES. This agreement is entered into between ____________________ (Contractor) and ____________________ (Owner).

2. DATE OF AGREEMENT. This agreement is made between these parties on this ________ day of ________________, 19___.

3. INTENT. The intent of this document is to include all materials, labor, and services necessary for the complete and proper execution of the work, and the conditions and terms for payment.

4. MATERIALS. Except as otherwise indicated, the Contractor shall provide and pay for all materials, water, power, and tools needed to perform the work specified. Unless otherwise noted, all materials shall be new and of a quality equal to or exceeding that listed on attached blueprints.

5. PERMITS AND REGULATIONS. The Contractor is responsible for obtaining and paying for any permits and licenses needed in order to start work. The Contractor shall comply with all local, state, and federal laws pertaining to the work and shall notify the owner if the drawings or any other item are at a variance therewith.

6. COMMENCEMENT AND COMPLETION. The work to be performed according to this contract will be started on ________________, 19_____, and subject to authorized adjustments only, completion shall be no later than ________________, 19____. If the contractor fails to complete the work for any reason by the stated completion date, he/she shall pay the owner the sum of $________________ per day, as liquidated damages, for each and every day that the completion is late.

7. PROTECTION OF PEOPLE, WORK, AND PROPERTY. The Contractor shall adequately protect the public, the work, and all adjacent property, and shall be responsible for any damage due to his act or neglect.

8. CHANGES IN WORK. The Owner has the right to make changes in the work provided that said changes are in writing and the contract sum is adjusted accordingly.

9. CORRECTION OF WORK. The Contractor, and any subcontractor hired by the Contractor, shall re-execute any work that fails to meet the conditions of this contract at no cost to the Owner. The Contractor shall also remedy any defects in materials or workmanship that appear within one year from the date of completion of the work at no cost to the Owner.

10. CONTRACT SUM. The Owner will pay the Contractor in cash, certified check, or money order for the performance of the work, subject to additions and deductions that have been agreed to in writing by both the Owner and the Contractor, the contract sum of $ ____________.

11. PROGRESS PAYMENTS. The Owner will make progress payments to the Contractor on account of the contract sum as follows:

Event	Amount of Payment
________________________________	______________
________________________________	______________
________________________________	______________
________________________________	______________

12. THEFT OF MATERIALS. The Contractor shall protect against and be responsible for the theft of any and all materials from the job site.

13. CONTRACTOR'S LIABILITY INSURANCE. The Contractor must maintain insurance to protect him and the Owner from claims under worker's compensation acts, from claims for damages because of bodily injury or death, and from claims for property damages due to the actions of the Contractor, a subcontractor, or anyone directly or indirectly employed or hired by either of them. Proof of this insurance must be provided to Owner before any work begins.

14. APPROVAL OF SUBCONTRACTORS. The Contractor must submit the names of all subcontractors to the Owner for the Owner's approval prior to hiring them. The Owner has the right to refuse the hiring of any subcontractor provided he has reasonable grounds for doing so.

15. CLEANING UP. The Contractor is required to keep the premises free from accumulation of rubbish by removing such at the end of each work day. Upon completion of the work, the Contractor shall remove all rubbish and waste material and leave the premises broom-clean.

16. TERMINATION OF THIS AGREEMENT. The Owner has the right, after five (5) days' written notice, to terminate this agreement if Contractor's work performed is not satisfactory.

17. FINAL PAYMENT. The final payment, constituting the complete unpaid balance of the contract sum, shall be paid by the Owner to the Contractor after the work has been completed, the contract fully performed, and the delivery to the Owner of a signed release of the mechanics' liens by the Contractor and all subcontractors and material suppliers.

Agreed to:

________________________________ ______________
Owner Date

________________________________ ______________
Contractor Date

________________________________ ______________
Witness Date

3. CONTRACTORS

Included in this appendix is a state-by-state listing of contractors who specialize in deck construction. They can help you with any aspect of your deck project, from design to completion.

Alabama

Berry Services
Birmingham, AL
(205) 822-0398

Custom Swearingen Fence & Deck Co.
Montgomery, AL
(205) 271-3121

Decks and Grills Inc.
Hoover, AL
(205) 979-0109

Decks, Etc.
Montgomery, AL
(205) 834-8666

Evans Home Improvement Inc.
Birmingham, AL
(205) 780-1781

Leisure Deck Builders
Wetumpka, AL
(205) 567-6433

Arizona

Dalcon Construction Inc.
Tempe, AZ
(602) 275-8423

Kerry Construction Company
Phoenix, AZ
(602) 861-8401

MFlex Corporation
Scottsdale, AZ
(602) 481-9886

Phoenix Patio Systems
Tempe, AZ
(602) 820-7732

Solar Structures of Arizona
Phoenix, AZ
(602) 951-9222

Arkansas

Burnett's Fence & Deck Company Inc.
Little Rock, AR
(501) 771-2456

Decks 'N Accessories Inc.
Little Rock, AR
(501) 565-0151

The Fresh Look Inc.
Little Rock, AR
(501) 821-2407

California

A-1 Builders
San Diego, CA
(619) 549-2116

C & M Builders
Huntington Beach, CA
(714) 848-5543

Caliente Redwood Decking
La Mesa, CA
(619) 461-1483

L A Decks
Whittier, CA
(213) 275-1685

Nor-Cal Decking Inc.
San Jose, CA
(408) 377-7702

R.L. Hayes Construction Company
Long Beach, CA
(213) 591-4399

Studio Deck
Beverly Hills, CA
(213) 744-0722

Sunset Designers & Builders
Long Beach, CA
(213) 424-0771

Colorado

Arapahoe Construction
Littleton, CO
(303) 796-0345

Colorado Deck & Fence Co.
Wheat Ridge, CO
(303) 423-4211

Colorado Decks & Patios Inc.
Thornton, CO
(303) 289-4268

Colorado Redwood Decks
Denver, CO
(303) 693-6244

Denver Decks
Denver, CO
(303) 367-2411

K & H Construction Company
Arvada, CO
(800) 348-8289

Connecticut

Archadeck
Marlborough, CT
(203) 295-8801

Archadeck
Old Greenwich, CT
(203) 698-0111

Decks by Stanley
Old Greenwich, CT
(203) 637-3483

Putnam Decks
Stamford, CT
(203) 323-2070

Upright Construction Company Inc.
Norwalk, CT
(203) 847-1402

Woodlake Construction Corp.
Stamford, CT
(203) 348-7634

Delaware

All Decked Out Inc.
Wilmington, DE
(302) 475-3300

Brandywine Services Inc.
Newark, DE
(302) 366-0880

Delmar Decks by Design
Wilmington, DE
(302) 738-3106

Holman Enterprises
Delaware City, DE
(302) 836-4043

Kustom Woodworking
New Castle, DE
(302) 322-3393

District of Columbia

A.B. Wilson, Inc.
Washington, DC
(202) 347-5553

Class Construction Corp.
Washington, DC
(202) 338-2564

Florida

Creative Decking
Orlando, FL
(407) 839-3466

Deck Builders
Apopka, FL
(407) 299-2481

Florida Custom Decks
Orlando, FL
(407) 649-9386

Mid-South Fence Co.
Orlando, FL
(407) 291-6015

Reynolds Carpentry & Construction
Apopka, FL
(407) 889-8111

Southern Garden Ponds
St. Petersburg, FL
(813) 541-5438

Wood Wizard Unlimited
Clearwater, FL
(813) 595-5853

Georgia

Archadeck
Atlanta, GA
(404) 303-9600

Archadeck
Macon, GA
(912) 742-1864

Archadeck
Smyrna, GA
(404) 351-5855

BJ Construction Company
Lilburn, GA
(404) 564-8788

Custom Home Improvements Company
Lawrenceville, GA
(404) 921-4453

Tech Builders Inc.
Atlanta, GA
(404) 633-3940

Idaho

Boise Deck Design & Construction
Boise, ID
(208) 378-4221

Briscoe Builders Inc.
Meridian, ID
(208) 888-1544

Pyramid Builders Inc.
Boise, ID
(208) 336-5505

Redwood Builders of Idaho
Garden City, ID
(208) 385-0505

Illinois

Archadeck
Aurora, IL
(708) 896-3325

Archadeck
Crystal Lake, IL
(805) 455-3251

Archadeck
Park Ridge, IL
(708) 692-3325

Archadeck
St. Joseph, IL
(217) 469-7230

Archadeck
Willow Springs, IL
(708) 839-8777

Deckmasters Plus
Chicago, IL
(708) 442-7999

Indiana

ABC Construction
Indianapolis, IN
(317) 255-5545

Archadeck
Angola, IN
(219) 665-7185

Archadeck
Brownsburg, IN
(317) 852-9177

The Backyard Company
Carmel, IN
(317) 848-9839

M.K. Akin Landscape & Design Inc.
Noblesville, IN
(317) 846-8048

Iowa

A-1 Builders
Urbandale, IA
(515) 270-8345

Cedar Rapids Home Repair
Marion, IA
(319) 373-1429

Leisure Living Home Improvements
Cedar Rapids, IA
(319) 363-1202

Rosswood Industries Inc.
Marion, IA
(319) 373-0550

Sunrise Builders
Des Moines, IA
(515) 252-0262

Kentucky

Chris Allgeier Construction
Louisville, KY
(502) 458-0866

Dependable Home Improvements Inc.
Louisville, KY
(502) 491-8693

Facile Construction Inc.
Prospect, KY
(502) 228-3220

Jim Cannady Construction Inc.
West Point, KY
(502) 922-4525

Louisiana

Bayou Classic Builders
Gretna, LA
(504) 889-4301

Dave's Fence Company
New Orleans, LA
(504) 834-9161

Sundek Creative Decks
Kenner, LA
(504) 465-0962

Maine

Deck Specialties
Falmouth, ME
(207) 797-7722

New England Deck & Creative Living
Gray, ME
(207) 657-2424

RJ Builders
Westbrook, ME
(207) 854-2700

Superior Sundecks Inc.
Portland, ME
(800) 535-5833

Maryland

Archadeck
Easton, MD
(301) 820-7553

Archadeck
Gaithersburg, MD
(301) 258-0440

Archadeck
Solomons, MD
(301) 326-1121

Archadeck
Timonium, MD
(301) 560-0099

Hi-Tech General Contractors
Glen Burnie, MD
(301) 761-7077

Maryland Sundecks Inc.
Pikesville, MD
(301) 653-8800

Sears Custom Decks
Arbutus, MD
(301) 247-6606

Massachusetts

Chiuchiolo Building & Remodeling
Worcester, MA
(508) 795-7414

Decks by Sisson
East Orleans, MA
(508) 255-6743

Landmark Design Landscape
Chatham, MA
(508) 432-8683

Prefontaine Brothers Inc.
Auburn, MA
(508) 752-2301

Pro Decks
Boston, MA
(800) 776-3325

Michigan

Archadeck
Washington, MI
(313) 726-0905

Baltic Building Company
Redford, MI
(313) 533-6570

Yardworks Construction Company
Detroit, MI
(313) 563-7781

Minnesota

A & L Construction
New Hope, MN
(612) 540-0102

The Fence & Deck Company
Golden Valley, MN
(612) 544-3393

Great Scapes Inc.
Chanhassen, MN
(612) 934-4477

Gustner Construction
Minneapolis, MN
(612) 535-7214

Henjum & Hayes Inc.
Prairie, MN
(612) 934-4792

Mississippi

First Magnolia Builders Inc.
Jackson, MS
(601) 957-1372

Taylor Crest
Jackson, MS
(601) 956-6380

W.E. Gray Construction Company
Jackson, MS
(601) 355-3534

Missouri

A-1 Decking
St. Louis, MO
(314) 351-1691

Adam Woodworking
Armand, MO
(314) 776-5680

Archadeck
St. Louis, MO
(314) 965-2240

Continental Decks Inc.
Kirkwood, MO
(314) 822-8809

St. Louis Deck & Gazebo
St. Louis, MO
(314) 771-5144

Nebraska

Anderson & Sons Construction Company Inc.
Papillion, NE
(402) 339-0134

D.L. Sorys Construction
Omaha, NE
(402) 333-2917

Linhart Construction Inc.
Ralston, NE
(402) 339-6748

Nebraska Home Improvement
Omaha, NE
(402) 334-8888

Nevada

Econodecks
Reno, NV
(702) 747-7293

Otero Custom Builders
Las Vegas, NV
(702) 362-1956

Outdoor Innovations
Reno, NV
(702) 827-0223

New Hampshire

Archadeck
Strafford, NH
(603) 664-5400

New Jersey

Archadeck
Flemington, NJ
(201) 657-0333

Anastasio Construction Inc.
Harpswell, NJ
(609) 466-2263

Decotis Carpentry
Trenton, NJ
(609) 396-1021

Natural Wood Concepts Inc.
Vincentown, NJ
(609) 859-0903

Riverview Construction
Titusville, NJ
(609) 737-3959

New York

Apricot Deck & Gazebo Company
Greece, NY
(716) 271-2120

Archadeck
Clifton Park, NY
(518) 877-5416

Archadeck
Jordan, NY
(315) 689-6816

Custom Decks by Nino
Rochester, NY
(716) 865-5705

Decks Unlimited
Carmel, NY
(914) 228-1733

Exteriors by Terry
Rochester, NY
(716) 377-2580

Just Decks Ltd.
Thornwood, NY
(914) 741-2210

North Carolina

Alteri Builders
Harrisburg, NC
(704) 455-1142

Archadeck
Arden, NC
(704) 684-2552

Archadeck
Charlotte, NC
(704) 845-5411

Archadeck
Hampstead, NC
(919) 452-3325

Archadeck
Kernersville, NC
(919) 996-1568

Archadeck
Raleigh, NC
(919) 676-1600

Chisolm's Home Improvement
Charlotte, NC
(704) 537-4457

Deckbuilders Ltd.
Charlotte, NC
(704) 596-2579

Ohio

Archadeck
Ashland, OH
(419) 281-3325

Archadeck
Bath, OH
(216) 838-1110

Archadeck
Chardon, OH
(216) 635-0000

Archadeck
Fairborn, OH
(513) 235-2233

Archadeck
Fairfield, OH
(513) 874-9132

Archadeck
Rocky River, OH
(216) 331-6080

Archadeck
Worthington, OH
(614) 785-1910

Deckmasters
Columbus, OH
(614) 846-1970

Landartisans Inc.
Ostrander, OH
(614) 881-4190

Martin-Reis Inc.
Columbus, OH
(614) 863-9110

Oklahoma

Powers Carpentry
Oklahoma City, OK
(405) 348-2993

Wiseco Construction Inc.
Oklahoma City, OK
(405) 789-8358

Oregon

Bald Peak Woodworks
Hillsboro, OR
(503) 628-0894

JRW Construction
Portland, OR
(503) 656-7561

Pacific Designs NW
Milwaukie, OR
(503) 654-5171

Superior Deck & Gazebo
Portland, OR
(503) 254-8056

Pennsylvania

Archadeck
Eaglesville, PA
(215) 539-1484

Archadeck
Lima, PA
(215) 892-9160

Archadeck
McMurray, PA
(412) 942-3840

Archadeck
Ruffsdale, PA
(412) 722-3737

South Carolina

Archadeck
Clemson, SC
(803) 654-3619

Archadeck
Columbia, SC
(803) 788-6892

Archadeck
Isle of Palms, SC
(803) 886-5137

Tennessee

Archadeck
Knoxville, TN
(615) 523-0236

Archadeck
Chattanooga, TN
(615) 752-1761

Arm-Vel Group
Memphis, TN
(901) 754-2146

Hearn Construction Company
Germantown, TN
(901) 753-6300

Liberty Fence Company
Memphis, TN
(901) 682-9844

Texas

Ace Builders
Round Rock
(512) 255-4788

Austin Deck Company
Austin, TX
(512) 472-1639

The Home Doctor Inc.
Austin, TX
(512) 836-4816

Woodcraft Construction
Austin, TX
(512) 892-4576

Virginia

Archadeck
Charlottesville, VA
(804) 295-9100

Archadeck
Front Royal, VA
(703) 635-7227

Archadeck
Herndon, VA
(703) 709-7954

Archadeck
Lynchburg, VA
(804) 385-7968

Archadeck
Manassas, VA
(703) 791-6610

Archadeck
Midlothian, VA
(804) 379-3325

Archadeck
Virginia Beach, VA
(804) 495-3316

Wisconsin

Archadeck
Racine, WI
(414) 639-2882

Glossary

ABUTTOR—A neighboring property that shares a common boundary with your property.

ACTIVE INGREDIENT—An ingredient in a mixture that precipitates a chemical reaction. Water and cement are the active ingredients in a concrete mixture.

AESTHETICS—The principles of beauty; the factors that cause something to be attractive and appealing.

AGGREGATE — Hard substances, such as sand and stone, that are mixed with cement to form concrete.

APPEAL—The process of making a formal request to a governing body to grant an exception to the law.

ARCHITECT—A person who is highly trained in all aspects of building design, and who has passed certain standardized tests and received a license, relating to the science of designing buildings.

ARCHITECT'S SCALE — A three-sided instrument, used by architects and designers, that has several ratios of actual measurements to those used in scale drawings.

AUGER—A tool for boring holes in the ground, used by soil scientists and engineers to get a soil sample.

BALUSTERS—Vertical members of a railing that are smaller and not as strong as newels but are installed to prevent children from falling off a deck or stairway.

BATTERBOARD—A temporary system of posts and boards set up for the purpose of identifying the exact locations of foundations.

BEAM—A large piece of solid lumber supported by posts, which carries the weight of a structure.

BEVEL—A sloping edge or surface on a piece of wood.

BEVEL SIDING — Siding that is made from beveled boards.

BLADE—1) The flat cutting edge of a knife or chisel. 2) The removable metal part of a power tool, which does the actual cutting. 3) The part of a framing square that is 1 1/2 inches wide by 16 inches long.

BLIND NAILED—A method of nailing decking boards, usually through the edges of the boards, so that the nails are not visible when the project is complete.

BLUEPRINTS—A detailed set of plans.

BOCA—Building Officials and Code Administrators.

BOCA CODE—A set of building guidelines compiled and issued by BOCA.

BOW—A type of warp in which a board is bent from end to end along its flat surface.

BOX NAIL—A nail with a medium-thick shank and a large head, used in many aspects of construction.

BRICK MASON—A mason who is an expert at constructing with bricks.

BRIDGING—Boards nailed between joists to prevent them from twisting and to transfer the weight from one joist to others.

BRIGHT—A nail that has no protective coating on it.

BUILDER — A person who engages in building houses, garages, decks, etc., for a living.

BUILDING CODE—A set of minimum construction standards that are a matter of law when adopted by a municipality.

BUILDING DESIGNER—A person whose trade is designing houses, garages, buildings, etc., but who does not have an architect's license.

BUILDING INSPECTOR—A person whose trade is inspecting construction to ensure that it complies with building codes.

BUILT-UP STRINGER—A type of stringer in which the blocks that support the treads and risers are attached to it.

CAMBIUM—The part of the tree that produces the new ring of wood each year. It is located just beneath the bark.

CANTILEVERED DECK—A type of deck that includes an overhang, which projects out without support under the edge of the deck.

CARPENTER—A person whose trade is making or repairing wooden structures.

CAULKING GUN—A tool used to apply caulking, which is purchased in tubes.

CEMENT—A gray powder made from the burning of lime and clay together, which sets to a stone-like mass when mixed with water.

CHALK LINE—A tool used to make long, straight lines by the application of chalk with a string.

CHECK—Lengthwise grain separation or splitting, which usually occurs at the end of a board as a result of improper drying procedures.

CIRCULAR SAW—A type of power saw that cuts by spinning a circular blade.

CLEAR—A high grade of wood free from knots or defects.

CLEAR ALL HEART—A high grade of redwood, free from knots or defects, which has been cut out of the heartwood.

CLEAT—A small board attached to a stringer that is used to support the treads.

CLEAT STRINGER—A type of stringer on which cleats have been attached to support the treads.

CODE APPEALS BOARD — A quasi-judicial board that has been given the power to grant exceptions or variances to a particular code.

CODE ENFORCEMENT OFFICE—A municipal office that handles the administration of code enforcement.

CODE ENFORCEMENT OFFICER—A person hired by a municipality to ensure that codes are being complied with.

COLD JOINT—A seam in concrete caused by pouring the concrete at different times and allowing the first pour to set before the second is poured.

COMBINATION SQUARE—A small hand tool used to draw perpendicular lines on boards.

COMMON NAIL—A type of nail with a thick shank and large head used in many aspects of construction.

COMPRESSIVE — A type of force applied to wood, which pushes down on a board or set of boards.

CONCRETE—A mixture of cement, water, sand, and stone, used in construction.

CONIFER—The classification given to evergreen trees that keep their needles year round. Softwood comes from conifers.

CONSTRUCTION HEART — The third lowest grade of redwood out of four grades of heartwood.

CONTRACT—A formal binding agreement between people or groups, which includes a document outlining the terms of the agreement.

CORRIDOR—A passageway, especially from room to room.

COVENANT—A formal binding agreement usually included in a deed.

CROOK—A type of warp in which a board is bent from end to end along its edge.

CROSS-SECTION—A drawing or representation of the internal structure of something that has been cut crosswise.

CUBIC FOOT—The volume of a cube with sides 1 foot long.

CUBIC YARD—The volume of a cube with sides 3 feet long.

CUP—A type of warp in which a board is bent from side to side across its width.

CUTOUT STRINGER—A type of stringer in which the places for the treads and risers have been removed from a solid board.

DEAD LOAD—The weight of the materials used to build the structure itself.

DECIDUOUS—The classification given to trees that shed their leaves annually, from which we get hardwood.

DECK CLIPS—Clips that have been specially designed to attach decking boards to joists by fastening them on their edge and presenting no visible method of attachment.

DECKING—The horizontal boards that form the floor of a deck.

DEED—A printed legal document that transfers ownership or rights and includes the giver's signature.

DELAMINATE—The process of laminated layers becoming separated.

DRAFTER—A person whose trade is to make drawings, plans, or sketches.

DRAINAGE DITCH—A special trench made of crushed stone and pipe for the purpose of draining groundwater.

DRESSED—Lumber that has been planed.

EASEMENT—A legal right held by a person to use the land of another.

ELECTRICIAN—A person whose trade is dealing with electricity or electrical equipment.

ELEVATION—The height of something, such as a deck.

ELEVATION DRAWING—A plan or drawing showing one side of a structure.

ENGINEER—A person who has been trained and is skilled in a branch of engineering.

ENGINEERING—The application of scientific knowledge for the determination, control, and use of power.

EROSION—The natural process by which the surface of the land is worn away by water.

EXCAVATION CONTRACTOR—A contractor whose trade is digging, removing, placing, and grading the ground.

FASCIA—A long, flat board located at the eaves of a house and attached to the ends of the rafters.

FINISH NAIL—A thin-shank nail with a small head, which has minimal holding strength but is ideal for attaching decorative pieces to a structure.

FOOTING—The bottom-most part of a foundation, which supports the foundation itself.

FOUNDATION—The strong base, usually made of concrete, upon which a building sets.

FOUNDATION CONTRACTOR—A contractor whose trade is the building of foundations.

FRAMING SQUARE—A hand tool used by carpenters to draw perpendicular lines.

GALVANIZE—To place a zinc coating on nails, bolts, and other iron parts to protect them from rusting.

GENERAL CONTRACTOR—A person whose trade is contracting all aspects of building construction.

GREEN—1) A person who is new to a trade and inexperienced. 2) Lumber that has been recently cut and has a high moisture content.

GROUND—1) A conducting connection between an electrical circuit or electrical equipment and the earth. 2) A terminal to which the grounding element is attached.

GROUNDWATER — Water lying below the ground's surface.

GUSSET PLATE—A rectangular piece of wood or metal attached to two boards where they meet to strengthen the seam.

GUTTER—A trough or channel under the eaves of a building to remove rainwater.

HANDRAIL—The top piece of a railing that is grasped and held onto for support as one goes up or down a stairway.

HARDWOOD—A general term that applies to all species of wood from deciduous trees.

HEAD—The round, flat part of a nail at the top of the shank, which is hit with a hammer to drive the nail into the wood.

HEADER—A piece of lumber in the framing of a structure that runs perpendicular to, and is attached to, the joists.

HEARTWOOD—The dense inner part of the tree that is not living.

HIGH-LEVEL DECK—A deck that has a surface more than 30 inches above the ground.

HYDRATION—The process of chemically combining a substance with water.

IMPACT LOAD—A type of live load placed on a structure that happens suddenly, such as the stress from a tree falling.

INERT INGREDIENT—An ingredient in a mixture that does not chemically react to or combine with other elements in the mixture. Sand and crushed stone are inert ingredients in concrete.

JOIST—One of the parallel boards in the substructure of a deck to which the decking is attached.

JOIST HANGER—A metal device used to attach a joist to a header or beam.

JOIST HEADER—The header that is attached to the ends of joists.

KILN—A very large oven used for drying lumber.

KILN-DRIED—The term that describes lumber that has been dried in a kiln.

KNOT—Branches that became embedded in the wood as the tree grew and that have been cut through when the log was sawed into boards.

KNOTHOLE—A hole in a board that exists because a knot became loose and fell out.

LAG SCREWS—Strong screws used for fastening boards together; they have six-sided heads, which can be screwed in by using a wrench or socket.

LAMINATE—To bond together by attaching several thin layers of a material.

LAMINATED BEAM—A beam that is made by attaching several boards together.

LANDING—The floor at the top or bottom of a set of stairs. This term is occasionally used to describe a platform.

LANDSCAPE ARCHITECT—An architect who is trained in all aspects of landscape design.

LANDSCAPE DESIGNER—A person who is trained in all aspects of landscape design but does not have an architect's license.

LATHE—An electrical tool used to turn wood and shape it by putting a cutting tool against the wood as it rotates.

LEVEL—1) A line, plane, or surface that is horizontal. 2) A tool used to check the horizontal plane of a structure.

LIEN—The legal right to another person's property until a debt owed in respect to it is paid.

LIEN WAIVER—A legal document granted by someone, usually a contractor, that ensures a lien will not be placed against one's property.

LINEAR—Of or pertaining to a line or length.

LINEAR FEET—The length in feet of an object, not taking into consideration its width or thickness.

LIVE LOAD—Forces or weight applied to a surface.

LUMBER—Timber sawed into planks or boards.

MASON—A person who builds or constructs with stone or brick.

MASONRY—Work that has been constructed by a mason.

MASON'S HOE—A tool used by a mason's helper

to mix mortar.

MICROCLIMATE—The climate of a very small area, such as a portion of one's yard.

MOISTURE CONTENT—The amount of water, expressed as a percentage, contained in wood.

MORTAR—A mixture of cement, water, and sand used by masons for building with brick or stone.

MULTI-LEVEL DECK—A deck that has two or more surfaces on different horizontal planes.

NAIL APRON—An apron with pouches, worn by a carpenter around the waist to hold nails.

NAIL SET—A tool used by a carpenter to drive the heads of nails below the surface of the wood without leaving a hammer indentation.

NEWEL—A large post usually located at an end of a railing or at the location that a railing angles. This post is what stiffens the railing and gives it strength.

NOMINAL—In name only but not in actuality.

NOSING—The projection of a stair tread beyond the front edge of the riser.

OUTCROPPING—A piece of ledge or bedrock that projects above the surface of the ground.

OVERHEAD—The structural part of a deck that is above one's head.

OUTLET—A device in an electrical wiring system that dispenses current when a plug is inserted.

PAINTER — A person whose trade is painting buildings or other structures.

PARTITION—A structure or wall that divides a room or space.

PENNY—A measure used to describe the different sizes of nails, which is abbreviated "d".

PERPENDICULAR — Coming together at right angles.

PHILLIPS SCREW—A screw with two perpendicular slots in the head.

PIER—A type of precast concrete foundation.

PILOT HOLE—A hole that is drilled into wood or metal before attaching with a screw.

PITCH POCKET—An opening in wood, usually between the growth rings, which contains a large amount of resin or pitch.

PLAN VIEW—A drawing from the perspective of being directly above the structure.

PLATFORM—The flat, level intermediate area between two parts of a flight of stairs.

PLUMB—Exactly vertical.

PLUMB BOB—A tool used to determine a plumb position.

PLUMBER—A person whose trade is to install or repair water pipes, drainpipes, etc., in or on a building.

PLYWOOD—Sheets of wood that have been made by fastening several thin layers of wood together.

PNEUMATIC—Operated by or filled with compressed air.

PNEUMATIC NAILER—A tool used by carpenters that drives nails automatically, using compressed air.

POST—A piece of wood or metal in a vertical position that supports some part of a structure.

POST ANCHOR—A metal device used to attach posts to foundations.

PRESERVATIVES — Chemicals or other substances used to protect wood from decay.

PRY BAR—A hand tool designed in a special way to give the user great leverage when prying.

PUBLIC HEARING—A meeting by a codes appeal board, in which the public is allowed to participate, to determine whether or not to grant an appeal.

RAILING—A horizontal structure built to protect against falling over an edge.

REPETITIVE LOAD—A type of live load that is placed on a structure a number of times, such as people walking across a deck.

RESIN—A naturally occurring substance, which

can also be made synthetically, used to make varnish, fiberglass, and plastics.

RESTRICTIONS — Limitations on building techniques and locations included in building and zoning codes.

RIGHT-OF-WAY — A path or route across another's land, which may legally be used.

RIM JOIST—Another name for a joist header.

RING NAIL—A nail with a series of rings on its shank, which gives it extreme holding power.

RISE—The total vertical distance from one step to the next.

RISER—The name given to the board nailed to the vertical face of one step.

ROOF DECK—A deck that is built upon the roof of a structure.

ROUGH—The term to describe lumber that has not been surfaced.

ROUGH OPENING—The opening in the framing of a structure into which a window or door will be placed.

RUN—The total horizontal distance from the front of one tread to the front of the next.

RUSTIC—Having a simple, unsophisticated, rough appearance.

SAFETY GLASSES—Special glasses that should always be worn when doing construction work to prevent wood chips and other similar fragments from entering one's eyes.

SAPWOOD—The living part of the tree located just beneath the cambium. This part of the tree carries water up to the leaves.

SAWHORSE — A rack that supports wood for sawing.

SCALE—The ratio of the actual measurements of an object to those of a drawing or model of it.

SCALE DRAWING—A drawing that is proportionate to something that has been or will be built.

SEASONING—The process of drying lumber.

SECTION VIEW—Another name for a cross-section.

SERVICE ENTRANCE — The electrical equipment that connects your house's wiring system to the local utility's electrical system.

SETBACK—The distance from a structure to the property line as required by the zoning ordinance.

SHAKE—A separation of the wood grain that does not penetrate the entire thickness of the board.

SHANK—The long, narrow, wiry part of a nail.

SHEAR — Lateral stress or pressure placed on a structure or board.

SHIPLAP—A board that has had its edges milled so that each board will overlap the preceding slightly.

SHRINKAGE — The amount that wood shrinks when it is dried.

SKETCH—A rough drawing of something that is not to scale.

SOFTWOOD—A general term that applies to all wood that comes from conifers.

SOIL ENGINEER — An engineer who has been trained in all aspects of soil science.

SOIL SCIENTIST—A person who has been trained in soil science and can make related evaluations but who does not have an engineer's license.

SONOTUBE—A round, hollow cylinder made of strong cardboard used for pouring foundation piers.

SPACING — The distance between centers of boards that run parallel.

SPAN—The distance between posts or points that support a beam.

SPECIAL EXCEPTION—A legal right granted by a codes appeal board to waive the code requirements in a particular instance.

SPECIES—A group of plants with common characteristics differing only in minor details from the others.

STATIC LOAD—A type of live load that remains constant, such as furniture.

STICKER—A small, thin piece of wood placed between boards in a stack to allow for air circulation during the drying process.

STONEMASON—A mason who is an expert at constructing with stone.

STRAPPING—Low quality strips of wood used as blocking or for nailing where they will not show.

STRINGER — The main board supporting the treads, the risers, and the load placed on the stairway by people and objects.

STRUCTURAL ENGINEER—An engineer who specializes in the design of structures.

SUBDIVISION—1) The division of a piece of land into three or more pieces within a five-year period. 2) A neighborhood developed by a developer.

SURFACED—A term synonymous with "dressed."

TAKEOFF—A material list made from a set of blueprints.

TAPE MEASURE—A hand tool, used by tradesmen for measuring, which has a retractable measuring element.

TEMPLATE—A pattern used as a guide for cutting exact replicas.

TENSILE — Resistance to breaking while being stretched.

TENSILE STRENGTH—The strength that a board has under tension.

TIMBER—Wood that has been prepared for use in building or carpentry.

TONGUE—1) The part of a framing square that is 2 inches wide and 24 inches long. 2) The part of a tongue-and-groove board that protrudes out in order to fit into the groove on an adjoining piece.

TONGUE AND GROOVE — A board that has been milled to have a tongue on one side and a groove on the other, so that it may interlock with other boards when placed together.

TORN GRAIN—The part of the wood that has been damaged by large machines that roll logs to remove their bark.

TOTAL RISE—The total vertical distance from the bottom to the top of a set of stairs.

TOTAL RUN—The total horizontal length of a stairway.

TRANSIT-MIXED CONCRETE—Concrete that is delivered by a large truck and is mixed while the truck is en route to the job site.

TREAD—The board that goes on the horizontal face of the step.

TRIANGLE — A tool, usually plastic, used by drafters in conjunction with a T-square, to draw parallel lines efficiently.

TRIM—Decorative pieces of wood on any project or structure.

TROWEL—1) A small hand tool used by masons to spread mortar. 2) The process of smoothing the surface of concrete as it hardens.

T-SQUARE—A tool used for drawing plans, which slides along the drawing board, allowing the user to draw parallel and perpendicular lines efficiently.

UTILITY KNIFE—A small, strong, razor-like knife used by and designed for tradesmen.

VARIANCE—A legal right granted by a codes appeal board to waive the code requirements in a particular instance.

VICTORIAN—Belonging to or characteristic of the period from 1837 to 1901.

WANE—An imperfection in a board caused by cutting boards too close to the outside of the log, resulting in a rounded edge that may or may not contain bark.

WARP—Timber that has bent because of uneven shrinkage or expansion.

WASHER—A flat ring placed beneath a nut or bolt to give it extra holding strength.

WINDER—A wedge-shaped tread located in a part of a stairway that turns.

WORKER'S COMPENSATION — Special insurance purchased by an employer to provide compensation to an employee in the event of a work-related injury.

ZONING CODE—A set of rules and regulations adopted by a municipality, which are a matter of law and must be complied with. Items such as noise, odors, traffic impact, density, lot sizes, permitted uses of property, and other similar items are usually regulated by the zoning code.

ZONING ORDINANCE — A term synonymous with zoning code.

Index

FIND THIS BOOK HELPFUL?
CHECK THESE OTHER USER-FRIENDLY TITLES* FROM BETTERWAY ...

The Complete Guide to Contracting Your Home, 2nd Edition — A Step-by-Step Guide for Managing Home Construction, by David L. McGuerty and Kent Lester. 288 pages, illustrations, forms, checklists. 1-55870-229-6. $18.95.

The Complete Guide to Residential Deck Construction—From the Simplest to the Most Sophisticated, by Greg Roy. 176 pages, photos (color and B&W), illustrations, forms. 1-55870-231-8. $16.95.

The Complete Guide to Buying Your First Home—Roadmap to a Successful, Worry-Free Closing, by R. Dodge Woodson. 216 pages, forms, glossary. 1-55870-228-8. $14.95.

Get the Most for Your Remodeling Dollar—How to Save Money, Save Time, and Avoid Frustration, by R. Dodge Woodson. 216 pages, photos, illustrations, checklists. 1-55870-211-3. $16.95.

The Complete Guide to Lumber Yards and Home Centers — A Consumer's Guide to Choosing and Using Building Materials and Tools, by Gary D. Branson. 176 pages, photos, illustrations. 1-55870-209-1. 14.95.

The Complete Guide to Floors, Walls, and Ceilings—A Comprehensive Do-it-Yourself Handbook, by Gary D. Branson. 176 pages, photos, illustrations. 1-55870-230-X. $14.95.

The Complete Guide to Barrier-Free Housing—Convenient Living for the Elderly and Physically Handicapped, by Gary D. Branson. 176 pages, photos, illustrations. 1-55870-188-5. $14.95.

The Complete Guide to Recycling at Home—How to Take Responsibility, Savce Money, and Protect the Environment, by Gary D. Branson. 176 pages, photos, illustrations. 1-55870-189-3. $14.95.

The Complete Guide to Remodeling Your Basement—How to Create New Living Space the Professional Way, by Gary D. Branson. 170 pages, photos, illustrations, checklists. 1-55870-162-1. $14.95.

The Complete Guide to Understanding and Caring for Your Home—A Practical Handbook for Knowledgeable Homeowners, by James Madorma. 272 pages, photos, illustrations. 1-55870-210-5. $18.95.

The Home Buyer's Inspection Guide, by James Madorma. 176 pages, illustrations, forms, checklists. 1-55870-146-X. $11.95.

The Complete Guide to Landscape Design, Renovation, and Maintenance—A Practical Handbook for the Home Landscape Gardener, by Cass Turnbull. 192 pages, illustrations. 1-55870-208-3. $14.95.

The Complete Guide to Decorative Landscaping with Brick and Masonry, by Edward J. Heddy and Pete Peterson. 160 pages, photos, illustrations. 1-55870-145-1. $11.95.

The Complete Guide to Painting Your Home—Doing it the Way a Professional Does, Inside and Out, by Jack Luts and Pete Peterson. 160 pages, photos, illustrations, forms. 1-55870-119-2. $11.95.

The Complete Guide to Home Security — How to Protect Your Family and Home from Harm, by David Alan Wacker. 192 pages, photos, illustrations, checklists. 1-55870-163-X. $14.95.

The Complete Guide to Decorating Your Home — How to Become Your Own Interior Designer, by Rima Kamen. 288 pages, photos (color and B&W), illustrations. 1-55870-117-6. $18.95.

* All in the large, 8½ x 11 format.

Please try your favorite bookseller first. If all else fails, tell us what you want. Send the price of the book plus $2.50 for UPS shipping (for any number of books) to Betterway Publications, Inc., P.O. Box 219, Crozet, VA 22932.